Twenty Black Years in the White Man's Military

Twenty Black Years in the White Man's Military

George E. Gurley, Sergeant, Retired, United States Air Force

VANTAGE PRESS
New York

FIRST EDITION

Published by Vantage Press, Inc.
516 West 34th Street, New York, New York 10001

Manufactured in the United States of America
ISBN: 0-533-13398-X

Library of Congress Catalog Card No.: 99-97496

0 9 8 7 6 5 4 3 2

Contents

Introduction vii

One Military Memories; Camp Lee, Virginia; Camp Stoneman, California 1
Two Hawaii; Korea; Japan; Camp Kilmer, New Jersey 20
Three Lackland Air Force Base; Cheyenne, Wyoming 32
Four Germany; Tierra Amarilla, New Mexico; Winslow, Arizona 40
Five Thule, Greenland; Anchorage, Alaska; Homer, Alaska 75
Six Philippine Islands, Vietnam, Thailand 86
Seven Westover Air Force Base, England; Torrejon AFB, Spain 104

Introduction

This book is dedicated to my late father and mother, George Gurley Sr. and Otelia Gurley, who instilled in me at an early age, the courage, stability, independence, and black pride that have been my trademark against seemingly overwhelmingly odds during my twenty years of service in the United States Armed Forces.

I am only speaking as one African-American regarding my racial encounters during my worldly travels as a United States Military man. I have experienced many racial incidents during my past military career. I have tried not to write this book as a one-sided point of view because many of my associates I met later on in the military were both black and white, and they were also bad and good. I am also looking at these incidents through a black man's eyes.

I truly hope and strongly recommend that the information contained in this book should be made known to all persons in America, regardless of race, creed or color and especially to the African-American youths who are our future leaders. Many of the racial incidents I experienced in the military are probably just a drop in the bucket compared to what has happened to many of my black brothers and sisters during this same period. I am keenly aware that there were many racial incidents experienced by African-Americans serving in the United

States Military. I am also aware that there were several other countries around the world where African-Americans serving in the United States Military experienced racial incidents.

My main purpose for writing this book is primarily because I believe that someone should keep a record of these incidents and document this information for future generations to comprehend and perhaps find a solution to this ugly problem. Although many of my black brothers and sisters would rather forget about those racial incidents or act as though they never happened, I can only say that I have forgiven people for some of the racial incidents I have experienced, but I will never forget them. I hold nothing personally against those African-Americans for their opposite views to my point of view because we are all individual thinkers. However, it is my belief that although racial incidents are presently materializing on and off of many United States military camps and bases around the world, many African-Americans still fear that they will be subject to criticism and reprisal if they mention anything in reference to racial discrimination.

Twenty Black Years in the White Man's Military

One

Military Memories; Camp Lee, Virginia; Camp Stoneman, California

This is a true story of my experience as a young eighteen-year-old black youth who volunteered to serve his country by joining the U.S. Armed Service on March 25, 1946 and served faithfully until my retirement on December 1, 1969. Many of the names mentioned in this story have been changed to protect the innocent.

I remember joining a segregated Army in 1946 because I believed that this was the only place a black man could go to make an honest dollar and be respected. I remember riding in the back of segregated buses and trains, eating in segregated lunch rooms, and sleeping on segregated military bases. I also remember the names and see the faces of many of my black buddies who were killed and maimed in Korea in that same segregated Army.

I remember receiving an Honorable Discharge from the United States Army in 1949, and thinking that this would be all I needed to be accepted into the mainstream of American society. I remember when I was hired as a messenger in the District of Columbia government and being told by my black supervisor that, “If you keep your mouth shut, one day you will be a messenger supervisor.”

I remember during the month of October 1952 that I became so disgusted with my future possibilities in the District Government, due to the lack of promotions, I joined the so-called Integrated United States Air Force. I remember after my induction into the Air Force, I was shipped to Lackland Air Force Base, located in San Antonio, Texas. I vividly remember one day while stationed on this base, I was put in charge of an integrated squad marching back from the dining hall, I asked one of the white recruits to keep in step with the rest of the squad and he told me, “Nigger, I am going to put the Ku Klux Klan on you if you ever attempt to leave off of this base.”

I remember being stationed in Germany from 1953 to 1956 and being refused service in several German bars and restaurants because they said they did not want to serve niggers.

I remember after returning to the United States in 1956 and during my tour of duty in New Mexico, I visited a bar in Chama, New Mexico, and was told by one of the white patrons that I would have to leave because where he came from niggers and white folks didn’t socialize in the same places. I remember refusing to leave when he ordered me to. Later on after departing from the establishment, a gun was drawn on me by this same white man with intent to kill. I remember when the white sheriff arrived and followed the suspect and later recovered the gun, but he did not apprehend the man. I remember when I asked him why he did not arrest the man, he told me,

"Nigger, all you have to worry about is what time you are supposed to report to court Monday morning."

I remember the trial being held in a service station. I remember that the judge owned the service station, the accused worked for him, and the white sheriff who arrested the accused was the defense counsel for him during the trial. I remember the case being dismissed because the judge claimed that he did not believe that he had the authority to render a decision in that case. I remember the accused walking forward, picking up his weapon and ammunition from the judge, and walking out of the court a free man.

I remember my white commanding officer calling me into his office after the trial and telling me that he was going to call all of the black troops together for a meeting because he heard that there were some serious concerns among them because of the outcome of the trial. I remember that he wanted me to tell the black troops that the reason the white man was not convicted was that there was not enough evidence presented. I remember how I refused to tell the black airmen that lie. I remember that because of my refusal to tell that lie, a letter was drafted by my commanding officer and several other white officers and my first sergeant and mailed to my mother stating that I was a troublemaker and I was passing my dislike about the base on to young black airmen and if I continued to do this, I would no longer be a noncommissioned officer.

I remember and have documents to prove that I was a victim of unfair treatment on an air base in England because I spoke out against several white officers and non-commission officers who were not performing their military duty according to standard military operating procedures.

I remember and observed several bars and eating establishments in Korea, the Philippines, Thailand, Vietnam, Japan, England, and Spain attempted to and some succeeded in refusing to serve black United States military troops in their countries. Many of these racial incidents also occurred in the United States of America involving black Americans serving in the Armed Forces dedicated to protecting this country.

Camp Lee, Virginia

My experience in the United States Military began when I volunteered to join the United States Army on March 25, 1946. This was a period shortly after World War II, although the war was not officially declared over. I received my orders assigning me to Camp Lee, Virginia. After realizing that I would be receiving my basic training in a Southern town, I had a feeling of apprehension. I hated the South and everything it stood for. I had heard many stories from our elders about how blacks were castrated and lynched in the South and I never forgot them.

During my trip through the state of Virginia, I experienced a deep sick feeling in the bottom of my stomach as I observed the landscape and the plantation-style homes. I could not help but think about the thousands of black slaves who had died as a result of lynching and torture by their white slave masters. The more emotional I began to feel about those incidents, the more I began to ask myself, was I really prepared for this adventure. I realized that I was an outspoken black youth and I would be at the mercy of an all-white Southern jury if I encountered any trouble.

I finally arrived at Camp Lee, Virginia, to begin my eight weeks of basic training. The camp was located a few miles outside of Petersburg, Virginia, one of cities in the South where some fierce Civil War battles were fought. This was a segregated camp with white soldiers living on one side of the camp and black soldiers on the other side. My first impression of the camp was my vision of a huge plantation. It appeared as though blacks were purposely housed in the back of the camp out of view from the main activities on the camp. I only saw or observed white commission officers, but there seemed to be an abundance of black sergeants and corporals. Most of them were former combat soldiers and seemed to be highly professional. They constantly reminded us that we would have to prove that we were the best and we would not depart that camp until we had proven it to them.

During the first four weeks into basic training, I cursed myself a thousand times for volunteering. We were up at 5:00 A.M. in the morning, reported to formation in front of the barracks, released to go to breakfast and marched from sunup to sundown. I marched so much that when I went to sleep, I would dream about marching. You would clean your weapon daily, take it apart, and put it back together. If you dropped your weapon, you would sleep on the floor and your weapon would sleep in your bed. After you scrubbed your barracks for inspection and it did not pass according to your sergeant, you would have to do it all over again until it was perfect. When one soldier screwed up in your barrack, the entire barrack would have to pay the price.

I will never forget the time when a few of us were caught gambling in the barrack after the lights went out. The drill sergeant ordered everyone of us to fall out in formation in front of the barrack at twelve o'clock midnight with our overcoats and raincoats on with a full backpack on our backs and helmets on our heads. He ordered the corporal to march us over to the work shed with all of this equipment on to pick up our shovels.

After picking up the shovels, we were ordered to walk between the barracks and select a space to begin digging. We were ordered to dig a hole six-by-six and not to return to the barrack until we were finished. Many of us asked the corporal how would we know when it was deep enough because we did not have a ruler? He said, when the dirt start falling back in the hole on top of us, then we will know that it is deep enough. We dug all night until approximately 6:00 A.M. Some of the soldiers went into the boiler room and went to sleep, but I was afraid to take that chance because I was too afraid of what would happen if that digging was not completed. I also dug the deepest hole.

The first sergeant came out that morning waking the soldiers up in the boiler room and told all of us that we could go to breakfast after we shoveled the dirt back in the hole, and he wanted the ground to look as flat as it was before we started digging. When I finished putting the dirt back in the hole I dug, there was a big hump in the ground and I just could not make the ground any flatter. Just as I was figuring out how I was going to get this job accomplished, an old sergeant came over to me and said, "Son, if you want to get it flat, go and get yourself a bucket of water, pour it into the dirt, and stomp on it until it gets flat." I proceeded to do just that and it worked, but I missed breakfast that morning.

I was assigned to a quartermaster company, but it seemed as though we were taking more infantry training than quartermaster training. The drill sergeants were given nicknames by us and some of those names were, "Iron Jaw," "Captain Midnight," and "Bring-em-back Alive." These sergeants struck fear into the hearts of every young recruit stationed on that camp, including me. When they ordered you to run, you had better not ask them how far and when they would order you to give them some push-ups, you did not ask them how many. Whatever these drill sergeants would order you to do, you would try to do it without hesitation or asking questions. They would also remind you that if you did not approve of what they ordered you to do, you could always request an appointment to meet with one of them behind the woodshed to settle things in other ways. There was no one whom I knew of who accepted that invitation during my eight weeks of basic training.

If a recruit made a right turn during drilling session after the drill sergeant gave a command to make a left turn, that recruit was ordered to go deep into the woods, locate, and bring out the largest log he could find. After dragging the log out, he was ordered to put the log on his left shoulder. He then advised the recruit that when he learned his right turn from his left, only then, could he get rid of the log. I remember one day when it was so hot that it was scorching on the drill field and one of the recruits made a wrong turn during one of the drill sergeants' commands. The drill sergeant ordered this recruit to pick up a foot locker half filled with coal and place it on his shoulder. When the drill session resumed, the recruit fell out due to heat exhaustion and later died. The drill sergeant was indicted for abuse, given a court martial, and later jailed.

During different phases of basic training, many of us were picked for detail at the camp stockade. This detail consisted of guarding the prisoners while they picked up trash on the camp. I wasn't too excited about getting picked for this detail, because, first of all, you were reminded bluntly that if one of the prisoners escaped, you would have to serve their sentence if he was not caught, and secondly, there were rumors that some prisoners had escaped previously. We were marched down to the stockade and then we would form a line in front of the prisoners while they marched out.

We would be assigned several prisoners to guard, walking behind them with our weapons pointed toward the sky while they walked behind the trash truck emptying trash into their bags into the truck. Most of the prisoners looked rough and tough, and they could sense that most of these raw recruits had some fear within. They would make remarks like, "I am going to take your weapon from you when we get behind the barracks," or, "I am going to run away from this detail because I know you are not going to shoot me." Those guys really made you nervous because you did not want to serve their time if they escaped. They really kept you on your guard until you returned them to the stockade.

Many of us were allowed to visit the city of Petersburg during the course of our basic training. My three trips to that city convinced me that it was no place for me to go and I didn't belong there. The African-Americans living in the city were very warm and friendly, but the attitudes of some of the whites I encountered there were very unfriendly. When I confronted several of them for information or directions, I got the feeling that they were trying to tell you, "Listen, black boy, you might be wearing that uniform representing the United States of America, but we control the blacks living in this city and don't you forget it." When I was walking through a predominantly white section of town, I could feel the sensation of not being wanted in that area. It was that awful feeling of being an intruder trespassing into their segregated city and they not wanting you there. I would mostly observe those hostile whites, and wonder about their mentality, and ignore them.

Venturing into the section of town where many of the African-Americans mingled was quite a contrast from being in the white side of town. There were several black-owned bars and restaurants. The people were very friendly and courteous. I would often ask myself, how could these black people be so happy with so many hostile whites? The white police officers seemed to be forever present in this area and when they spoke to some of the black residents, it was always with an air of dominance. I would always stop and observe when these white officers would talk to some of the black residents. Most of them would smile and be polite to the officers regardless of the derogatory remarks they made. This would anger me very much because I knew within myself that it really hurt some of them inside to smile at these officers, but they were afraid and wanted to survive.

There were some black military policemen who were visible to check on military personnel. Some of them were just as bad or worse on black military personnel as their white counterparts. One black military policeman made his infamous reputation by beating a black soldier so severely with his nightstick when he thought he was being smart when he answered him. We called him "Big Red" because he was a big red black man. Even today, there are still military men living who were stationed in Camp Lee at that time and still hold a great hatred for this individual.

I finally received a three-day pass to visit my home in Washington, D.C. I thanked God for this relief because we had been promised a pass several times before, but someone would screw up in the barracks and passes would always be canceled. It was also nice to release some of the tension by seeing your relatives.

After enjoying my relaxation at home, just thinking about returning to Virginia caused excessive tension in my stomach. I just hated going back South and I felt it with a passion. When I arrived at the Greyhound Bus Station, I watched blacks arriving in Washington, D.C., with their possessions in bags, suitcases, and boxes. They were coming in from different parts of the South, and I was very happy for them. The faces on many of them gave me a feeling that they were tired, beaten, and looking for a better future. When the bus crossed the Potomac River and reached the Virginia side, it seemed as though all of the black people on the bus got quiet, making it seem as though they were headed for a destiny of doom.

We finally arrived in Richmond, Virginia, and the bus pulled in for a rest stop. The driver said that we would be there for a few minutes and we were allowed to get off and purchase refreshments. I was wearing my military uniform and I really didn't believe I would have any problems buying something to eat.

I entered by the main entrance to the bus station and waited for someone to take my order.

One of the white waitresses told me that I would not be allowed to order anything on that side of the station and I would have to go over to the other side if I wanted to be waited on. This request really hurt my pride more than my feelings. Although I was tempted to ask her why, I swallowed my pride and walked around to the other side. I felt as though I should not get into trouble while I was still going through basic training.

After reaching the other side of the bus station to purchase some food, I found the interior of the place looked deplorable. The floor was dirty and there was an opening on the side of the wall where the food was handed to you as if they were feeding a dog. Some of the black passengers were ordering food. I guess it was because they were used to this kind of treatment. I tried to understand to a certain degree, but I refused to buy anything. This was my first time experiencing this type of treatment and it really bothered me.

Although there was segregation in Washington, D.C. during the period when I was growing up there, I never experienced the treatment that I was receiving at this bus station. Sure there were restaurants, bars, and other establishments that only catered to whites. But then again, I never desired to eat or socialize with whites during that period because there were so many black establishments in the city where you could get a decent meal. It never bothered me. I can never remember riding on the back of a streetcar or bus in the District of Columbia just because I was black. During my early years, I never felt the degree of segregation that some blacks felt or experienced in other parts of the South. To me, it was more of the principle involved in that incident that caused my bitterness and frustration.

It was obvious to all of the black troops that the rigid basic training that we were receiving had molded us into a cohesive group of fighting men. When we started marching, all you could hear was the thick rubber heels on our boots digging into the black top road with precision. Everyone was in step and we could sense the feeling of pride and accomplishment as we marched in cadence. When we marched past a company of white soldiers on the road, the drill sergeant would holler out dig-em-in and the thud of our heels would be so loud that the white soldiers would get out of step. We would smile to ourselves and keep on marching.

During the last few weeks of basic training, we finally received the opportunity to put our training to practice under staged combat conditions. We boarded trucks and were driven to an area called AP Hill located a few miles from Camp Lee, Virginia. The story goes that this land belonged to an old man named Andrew Phillips and it was called a reservation. It was donated to the United States government by this old man who later died.

During our military exercise on AP Hill, we practiced attacking and capturing buildings with blank ammunition, learned how to knock out enemy tanks, and how to sleep in the woods after setting up our pup tents. During this military exercise, we were really feeling that we had reached the threshold of being the best trained soldiers in the world. Prior to arriving on AP Hill, many of the recruits were whispering amongst themselves about how they were going to get even with some of the drill instructors for being so hard on them during basic training. They were aware that it would be dark out there and we would be going on night problems and they figured this would be the exact time and location to carry out their plot.

One night while we were out on a night problem climbing a steep hill in the woods, someone threw a stick and hit one of the drill instructors in the eye. We were ordered to come to a halt and the instructor asked us who threw the stick. No one said anything, but I knew it was the guy behind me who threw it, but I wasn't talking. In fact, most of us were aware of who threw the stick, but no one was saying anything. After hearing no response from the troops, the instructor said we were going to rest for tonight and we were ordered to set up our tents for that night. He then ordered the five recruits behind me to remain in line until he returned.

After the instructor pointed out to the rest of the troops how he wanted the tents in the area to be set up, he returned to the troops he left standing in line. He ordered them to move approximately twenty feet away from the area where we were setting up our tents. He ordered them to reach in their back packs and get their spoons out of their mess kit (eating kits). They were then ordered to get down on their knees and start digging with their spoons. He said, "When you find out who threw that stick at me, only then will you stop digging and go to sleep." The next morning when we awoke, they were still digging with those spoons.

After the exercise ended, we boarded the trucks for our departure from AP Hill. We were a happy bunch of black recruits because we knew without a shadow of a doubt that we had finally completed eight hard weeks of basic training. We laughed, joked, and sang during the entire trip back to Camp Lee. One of the first things we did when we returned to camp was to go over to the barracks where the new recruits had arrived and were waiting to start basic training. We hollered at the top of our voices, "YOU WILL BE SORRY."

After the completion of basic training, most of us just lounged around the barracks trying to avoid being put on detail before we received our orders for a new assignment. During this period, one of the drill instructors entered the barracks one day and requested some volunteers for a detail. One of the first things I learned upon entering the military service was you never volunteer for anything. It seemed as though there were only a limited amount of volunteers, and with my bad luck, I was selected to join the detail.

On the way to the detail location, the instructor

asked us how many of us could swim. Not realizing what I was about to get into, I raised my hand along with a few of the other recruits. After marching to the other side of the camp, we were asked to form two groups, one for the swimmers and one for the non-swimmers. The swimmers were told to pick up swimming trunks in the shed and jump into the swimming pool and the non-swimmers were ordered to start picking up trash around the entire area. While we were in the pool, we were given wash cloths to wipe the dirt and grease off of the side of the pool.

When I finally realized that this pool was used only by white troops, I really resented that and was furious about this detail. Although there might have been a pool for black troops, I can honestly say I never saw one and none of the black troops ever mentioned one being on the camp. It was hard for me to comprehend why they did not get white troops to do this little nasty detail.

I was eventually notified to report to personnel and receive my orders for my new assignment. When I reported to the office, I was disappointed to find out that my request to be assigned to the mounted cavalry was canceled and I would not be going to Germany as was promised. This news made me so angry that I wanted to get out of the Army immediately because I had been lied to twice. When I questioned why my two choices were canceled, I was told that the Army was disbanding the mounted cavalry and no more soldiers were being sent to Germany. I was later notified by the personnel office that I could accept one of two possible assignments: I could accept an assignment to Fort Jackson, South Carolina, or I could sign a waiver and be shipped to Southeast Asia. I was also told that I would have to make my choice as soon as possible because if no choice was made, I would automatically be assigned to Fort Jackson, South Carolina. I was allowed to go outside of the building for a few minutes to return my choice.

While standing outside of the building debating on where I would best go, I had a short discussion with an old black sergeant. I mentioned to him the choices personnel had offered me after my original choices were turned down. He said, "Son, they are probably going to disband the mounted cavalry, but the story about not sending anymore soldiers to Germany is a lie. What he should have told you was they are not sending too many more black soldiers to Germany because they don't want you mingling with those white women." He further stated, "Whatever you do, don't sign that waiver to go to Southeast Asia." I asked him why. And he said, "Son, the white man will send you to one of those islands over there and forget about you." I thought very seriously about what the old sergeant had told me, but I also realized my deep hatred for the South and the many atrocities committed against black people by whites in the South. I also heard many stories about the unfair treatment of black soldiers stationed at Fort Jackson, South Carolina. My final decision was that I would take my chances in Southeast Asia. Later, I received my orders instructing me to report to Camp Stoneman located in California.

Camp Stoneman, California

After spending my thirty-day furlough at home, I boarded a train at the Union Station in Washington, D.C. for my destination in California. This was my first long-distance trip to any place in the United States, and I did not realize that California was so far away. My mother gave me forty dollars and I thought this would be enough to last me until I arrived in California. This thought proved to be erroneous because when the train arrived in Chicago the next morning, I had spent all but five dollars of that money and found out that there were approximately three more days of traveling before we reached California.

When I departed Chicago, there was a friend of mine also going to the same base, so we pooled our little change together for the next three days and dined on bread and bologna until we reached Camp Stoneman. We arrived on base in the afternoon and we were so hungry after that long trip, we washed up and went straight to the dining hall. We really loaded our trays down with almost everything available to eat. I told my buddy that he had so much food on his tray that he could not see how to find a table.

After eating supper, we showered and went to the movie on base. The movie started around seven-thirty that evening and we were only in there about fifteen minutes and we watched as four or five soldiers began leaving the side exit going out of the theater. A short time later, we saw about ten soldiers running for the exit. I told my buddy that there must be something happening on the base for all of those soldiers to leave after only a short period in the movie. Before I could receive an answer from him, a pain hit me so hard in my stomach I had to get up and run for the exit with my buddy not far behind me.

I ran straight to the barracks to find the latrine. Every latrine was filled to capacity even those in the three other barracks that we visited. Everyone was moaning and groaning about how their stomachs were hurting. Some of the soldiers even fell on the floor. We all had a case of GI's and this happens when you eat from some of the trays that have not been washed properly leaving a lot of grease in them, and that is the end result. Many of us went on sick call, but we all felt better the next day.

I spent approximately three months on this base and during that time, we made several trips up to the top of a nearby mountain preparing for this trip overseas. Sometimes we would stay overnight on this mountain, and it was really cold at night. You would sleep in your fatigues and socks and put several blankets over you to keep warm. We were ordered to fire weapons on the rifle range. This type of action was somewhat of a mystery to some of us because none of the other troops were participating in this action. There were many rumors about where we were headed, but no one really knew what to believe. Some of the older soldiers who were permanent party on the base said that we were being sent where things were pretty hot and we had better know how to shoot. We were finally notified that we would be going to a country called Korea. In other words, we were on our way to South Korea to be assigned to the United States occupation forces.

We sailed from San Francisco on a ship named the *Chanute Victory*. This was one of those victory ships that was used during most of the war carrying troops and supplies to help the war effort. Our first stop on this voyage was Hawaii. We reached Hawaii within a few days. During my first few hours on this ship after leaving San Francisco, I went below deck down to our quarters to get my field jacket because it was a little breezy. After getting my jacket to return to the deck, I got so seasick that I had to stay below deck until the next day. Not only me, but several of us were moaning and groaning and running to the toilet.

Two

Hawaii; Korea; Japan; Camp Kilmer, New Jersey

Hawaii

When we reached Hawaii, most of us stayed on ship overnight. However, some of the troops were allowed to get off of the ship for a few hours to do a little shopping and sightseeing. I was not one of the lucky ones. When the troops returned to the ship, many had purchased pineapples and coconuts. Some of the black troops said that they were not given a very warm welcome when they went into town. Some said that they were glad to get back on the ship.

We departed for Korea the next day. I remember vividly when the ship departed from Hawaii because I glanced over the back railing of the ship (I believe the sailors refer to it as "the fan tail" of the ship), and observed about twenty to thirty sharks following the ship. I believe some of the sailors were dumping garbage over the back. I could just imagine what would have happened if someone were pushed or fell off of the ship.

During this long trip to Korea, many of us were assigned specific details on the ship. I spent most of my time working in the bakery shop making bread and scrubbing floors. This trip took approximately three weeks, and we saw nothing but water during our first couple of weeks. I remember one day when I heard a lot of commotion out on the deck and went to see what was happening. Someone had spotted a little object that looked like it was about five hundred miles away and they were just waving. It was another ship, but it was so far away you could barely make out what it was. We only knew that we had seen something else besides water.

There was something else I noticed on this ship. There were about six or seven Air Force guys on this trip and every day when I would see them, they were sunbathing on the ship and reading books. It seemed as though they never had any work to do. It was only the Army personnel that was doing the work. I said to myself at that time, If I ever came back into service, it would be in the Air Force and not the Army.

Korea

We arrived at the port of Inchon, Korea, during the month of August 1946. We arrived at night and when looking at the city of Inchon at night, it was a beautiful sight. It reminded me of looking up at the hills in California at night with all the lights on. We were notified that there would be no disembarkation at night due to the low tide in the Inchon harbor. We slept on board the ship overnight. As we prepared to leave the ship the next morning, I saw the city of Inchon for the first time during daylight hours. What I observed was a dullish grayish look, and I remembered remarking to my buddies as to how the night and city lights could fool you.

We boarded the landing barges and headed for shore with our helmets on and carrying our empty weapons. There was a large contingent of black soldiers on board prior to our landing on shore. When we began unloading on the dock, many of the Korean people, seeing all of these black soldiers and some of them seeing blacks for the first time, went into a panic situation and some began running away from us. We smiled because we kind of expected this type of reaction. I remember one specific incident when the train was pulling into the train station for the troops to load on, and the black troops were marching in formation to get to the train and load on. This Korean youth about seventeen or eighteen years old panicked after seeing us moving towards him and was in such a hurry to get out of the way that he was struck by the train. Some of the train officials went to his aid, but we never found out what happened to him later.

Although we had unloaded off of the barges in Inchon that morning, we did not arrive at our destination at Yong Dong Poe until late that night around 10:00 P.M. One of the reasons it took so long was that the train would go so many miles forward and back up so many miles. I believe the distance between Inchon and Seoul, Korea, was approximately twenty-three miles. Yong Dong Poe was about a mile from the bridge into Seoul. After processing at Yong Dong Poe for about three or four days, we were finally loaded on to trucks, driven across the bridge into Seoul, and unloaded on to a small camp across the road from the Seventh Division Headquarters. We were members of the Twenty-Fourth Corp. We wore a patch on the shoulder shaped like a heart with the colors of purple and white.

I was assigned to a gasoline supply company. The black troops assigned to this company would eat breakfast around 6:00 A.M. in the morning. After breakfast we would load onto trucks for a ride to the Army gasoline supply dump located near the train yard in Seoul. We would unload off of the trucks and start the day rolling and loading fifty-five gallon drums of gasoline on trucks waiting for pickups. At lunch time we would stop work load up on the trucks and go back to the base for lunch. After lunch we would load up on the trucks and return to the gasoline dump to roll and load more drums of gasoline until quitting time. This was our daily routine five and sometimes six days a week. This was extremely hard work, and when we returned to the base, after supper meal, we would head straight to our bunks.

On some weekends, we were at certain times allowed to visit downtown Seoul. I can remember many of the Korean adults and kids laughing and pointing at us as though we were something from outer space when we walked down some of the streets. It did not bother me so much when the kids would do that, but I could not comprehend why the Korean adults would do it. There was this street named Bong Chong Street, and it seemed as though this was the area where most of the dance halls and bars were located. I spent most of my time sightseeing because I did not want to get insulted while visiting those establishments. Some of the black soldiers would go into those bars and challenge those who made fun of them. There were rumors, and only rumors, that a group of black soldiers were insulted downtown and went back to the base and got guns and ammunition, returning and shooting up a couple of bars.

Most of the black soldiers did not socialize with the white soldiers, and most of the white soldiers did not socialize with black soldiers. There were exceptions to the rule, but in general, it was still a segregated Army, even though we were all Americans overseas fighting for the same cause.

During the period when we were working at the gasoline supply dump, many North Koreans were infiltrating into South Korea to sabotage and disrupt normal operations in the southern part of the country. These were dangerous times for all of us during this period. I remember one day when we were working at the gasoline supply dump, we heard gunfire over in the train yard almost adjacent to where we were working and it was very clear to us that there was house to house fighting between the South Korean police and possibly North Korean infiltrators. We left the gasoline supply dump to return to the base for lunch.

When we arrived on the base, the duty sergeant reported to the commanding officer the scene that we had witnessed involving the gun fire. He requested that we should be armed with ammunition and weapons to defend ourselves prior to returning to work. We were ordered to report to the supply room to pick up our weapons, but we were not allowed to draw any ammunition. We loaded on the trucks and returned to work after lunch with empty weapons and no ammunition to defend ourselves.

It was hard for me and the rest of the troops to comprehend why these black troops were being sent back to work in hostile territory with empty weapons and no ammunition and they were fighting like hell in the train yard with live ammunition. It was again a rumor, but it could have been the truth; black soldiers were not to be trusted with live ammunition without white supervision.

We were notified one day that, if there was anyone interested in being transferred into an infantry outfit, he should report to the orderly room. Several of the black troops, including myself, reported to be transferred. We filled out several forms and were ordered to report to the supply room to pick up infantry gear and weapons. After receiving this equipment, we were placed in separate barracks from the other troops. About two days later, we were asked to fall out in formation and prepare to load up on trucks in full battle gear within twenty minutes and prepare to leave. We started loading up on the trucks and started out the front gate. We pulled into a convoy with hundreds of other trucks parked on this long road. The rumors started flying that the Russians were getting ready to cross the Thirty-eight Parallel and we were needed to stop them. I asked myself, *what in the hell have I got myself into?* When the convoy moved out about a mile, we stopped for about thirty minutes while there was a little discussion. Suddenly, the convoy made a u-turn and we returned to the base.

When we first landed in Korea for this occupation duty, we were told that we would only be there for six months. Even a famous radio commentator who was well respected in that field had stated that we would be leaving Korea very soon. Now it was getting to be almost a year since we arrived in that country and we were still there. I began to think about what that old black sergeant had said to me in Camp Lee, Virginia, when I made the choice of coming to Southeast Asia. He said, "That white man will send you to one of those islands and forget about you."

We were transferred from the infantry back into our Quartermaster Company. Our outfit departed from Seoul and arrived on a permanent base on the outskirts of Inchon. This base was located at the end of a long dusty road leading from the city of Inchon. It was surrounded by a tall wooden fence. It reminded you of the forts that were built by the settlers in the Western part of the United States when they were protecting themselves from the Indians during the nineteenth century. There were guards stationed at the gate twenty-four hours a day. The living quarters for the black soldiers were located near the front of the base and the living quarters for the white soldiers were located in the rear of the base. We were all living in Quonset huts and when it got too hot under the tin on the roof, it felt as though you were baking inside. In the wintertime, it seemed as though it would get so cold, it would freeze the diesel we were burning. We would go from one extreme to the other.

Many of the troops felt better about being transferred to this base, but many of us were getting a little disgusted about our situation. There were many reasons as to why many of the black troops were getting frustrated. First of all, we did not feel as though we were being treated as equals to white soldiers and secondly, the work assignments we received were always hard labor. Many of us believed that working on the plantation during slavery time was the same on our base as it was then. And to make matters worse, we soon learned that our next job assignment would be working on a larger gasoline supply dump in Inchon. This was a major gasoline supply dump that received all drums of gasoline unloaded off of the ships in the harbor and distributed them throughout the command in that area. This was hard to take, but we tried to take a bad situation and make it a positive one. We were all young strong black soldiers and we would always say "Let's take a day at a time."

The company was run by a white commanding officer and he had a black first sergeant. During our first two weeks on the base, the weather was extremely hot and when we went to eat at the dining hall (mess hall), the windows were left opened due to the very hot atmosphere. Every few minutes, a little breeze would blow through the open window and there would be a foul odor in the air. Each soldier would begin to look at one another, believing that someone was smelling. We were finally advised by some of the older soldiers that the smell was coming from some of the Korean farms located around the camp. They pointed out that Korean farmers used human waste to fertilize their farms, and they would store this waste in a hole and then stir it up when they began to use it to grow their crops. This was a terrible smell, but they seemed to grow healthy green food on their farms. They would haul this stuff through the streets with an ox pulling the cart. We used to call them the honey buckets.

We finally began to mingle with some of the Koreans living outside of the base. At first, some of them were apprehensive about socializing with us because the Korean police told them if they were caught in the company of black soldiers, they would be put into jail. The Korean police also told them if they mingled with white soldiers, they would not treat them as badly as they would be treated if caught with black soldiers. Many of the Koreans said the white soldiers had told them that black soldiers were sent over there to fight at night and they fought during the day. There were many undernourished Koreans and many living in poverty with hardly anything to eat. The black soldiers started buying food for some of the sick and disabled Koreans and looking out for the children.

When the word got around about how nice and kind we were, there would be many Korean women and children waiting outside of the base for us when we got off of duty. This was a far cry from the reception we got from some Koreans when we black soldiers got off of the ship. I also noticed that those Koreans living in the rural areas were more friendly than those living in the city. We understood that Korean customs and beliefs were very rigid when it involved associating with other nationalities. However, all Koreans did not follow those customs and beliefs.

I was notified by the first sergeant that I would be assigned to the orderly room to be the company mail clerk. I don't know why I was picked to be the mail clerk, but I was not complaining. After my sweating and getting sore muscles from rolling and lifting those fifty-five gallon drums of gasoline and diesel, that news was good news.

Several weeks later, I was asked whether I would like to go on a ten day furlough to Japan. My reply was a big yes. I knew several other soldiers were being selected to go on some of these trips, but it was a complete surprise when I was asked to go.

We boarded the train in Inchon for our trip across Korea to the port of Pusan. When we arrived in Pusan, we departed the train and loaded on to a small boat located in the harbor. During this voyage across the Sea of Japan, the water was choppy and very rough. Most of the soldiers on the boat were seasick during the entire trip.

Japan

After landing in Japan, we boarded a train headed for Osaka, Japan. After arriving there, we boarded a bus for a short ride to our hotel, located a little outside of Osaka. When we reached the hotel, we found it was a huge beautiful building surrounded by manicured lawns. There were many Japanese bellhop boys, waiters and waitresses to greet us. We did not have to lift a finger to do anything.

As usual, while walking through town or visiting the parks, being a black man, you were the center of attraction. There was a beautiful park a short walk from my hotel, and I would spend most of my time sitting in that park admiring the gorgeous flowers and trees and watching the waterfalls.

One day during one of my walks through the park, I met a beautiful Japanese girl and we struck up a conversation. She was very curious about black people and I was very curious about Japanese people. She spoke a little English and I spoke a little Japanese.

I would meet with this Japanese girl during the rest of my leave in Japan and we really enjoyed each other's company. On many occasions we would have to hide behind trees and buildings in order to keep from being seen by some Japanese people. She expressed concern to me that her family would do something bad to her if they knew she was talking to a black man. On the other hand, she said many Japanese people did not have a big problem talking to or socializing with white soldiers. Prior to my leaving for my trip back to Korea, we met in the park for our last time together. We embraced, wished each other the best of luck, and parted.

During the middle of 1948, we were notified that we would be leaving Korea for good. We were some happy troops because we had stayed much longer than we were expected to in that country and now we were getting the opportunity to leave. We were told that soldiers who had less than six months left on their tour of duty in the military would go back to the States and wait to be discharged and the other soldiers with more than six months left on their enlistment would be sent to Japan to be stationed in the Infantry.

Camp Kilmer, New Jersey

I departed Korea in August of 1948 and after a short leave at home, I was assigned to Camp Kilmer, New Jersey, until I received my Honorable Discharge in 1949.

After my discharge from the United States Army, I was hired as a messenger working for the federal government. I was continually told by my black supervisor that, "If you keep your mouth shut, one day you will be a messenger supervisor." After working as a civilian for approximately two years, I thought very seriously about going back into the military.

I finally decided to go to the recruitment office and take my United States Air Force examination and volunteer for military duty. I passed my written examination and my physical and was assigned to Lackland Air Force Base training center located in San Antonio, Texas.

Three
Lackland Air Force Base; Cheyenne, Wyoming

Lackland Air Force Base

I arrived at Lackland Air Force Base during the month of October 1952. Although integration of the Armed Forces had been made law by President Truman in the late forties, this would be my first experience living and sleeping in the same barracks with white military personnel. Truthfully speaking, I had a feeling of uneasiness because after living so many years in a black segregated environment, I just did not know what to expect from the whites. My first thoughts were, *How would I react if a white soldier called me a nigger?*

My first order of business when I entered the barracks that I was assigned to was to find a black face. There were none to be found at that time, so I choose to sleep on a top empty bunk between three white airmen. They tried to be friendly and so did I, but I could feel from the tension in the air that somehow we were all pretending. I knew that I did not want to be in the same area with them and they knew that they did not want me in their little area.

For the first two weeks, we coexisted. I kept my distance and they kept theirs. Due to the fact that I had prior military training in the Army, I automatically received one stripe and was given the position of squad leader in my barrack. There were approximately fifteen black airmen in the squadron and they were distributed evenly within each barrack.

During my third week of basic training, we really began to speak openly and became friendly with each other. I believe this was due to the rigid training and all the hell we were catching from our tact leader. We finally realized that we all had something in common and that was that we hated his guts. During a conversation one night in the barrack, I learned that the white airman sleeping on the bunk underneath me was from Alabama, the white airman occupying the bed on my right was from Tennessee, and the white airman occupying the bed on my left was from Mississippi. I said to myself, *What a hell of a combination of white men.* They all gave me due respect.

One night while lying on our bunks after a rough day in the field, the white airman from Alabama looked up from his bottom bunk and said jokingly, "Gurley, if my grandfather knew I was sleeping underneath a black man in the same barrack, he would turn over in his grave." We all laughed at his remarks, and I did not take it as an offense because *I knew he was sincere and he was also telling the truth.*

One of the most serious confrontations I experienced during basic training happened one day as I was marching ten airmen back from the dining hall after kitchen police duty (KP). All of the airmen were in perfect step, except this one white airman. I called the column to a halt, approached the airman, and asked him why he was unable to keep in step with the rest of the airmen. He refused to answer my question after I asked him several times. As I proceeded to walk away from him, he said, "Whenever you leave out of the front gate going to town, I am going to put the Ku Klux Klan on you."

Quite naturally this came as a shock to me, but I remained calm and told him that he was not in town now and I would advise him to keep in step with the rest of the troops. One of the white airmen stepped out of rank and said, "Gurley, don't get yourself in trouble; I will take care of him for you." I told him I appreciated his concern, but I could handle the situation. Later that night after duty, I was informed that this white airman from Boston, who had offered to assist me earlier during the day, had agreed to meet the airman involved in the incident behind the tents on the field for a fight. During the following weeks, I never encountered any more incidents with that individual and he was always in step with the rest of the troops.

Cheyenne, Wyoming

After completion of basic training at Lackland Air Force Base, I departed by plane to attend a communication school located at Francis E. Warren Air Force Base in Cheyenne, Wyoming.

This rugged state diversified in mountains, valleys, plains, and plateaus was one of the coldest places I had been stationed at in the States. I arrived during the month of January, and the wind was blowing so hard that you had to stand behind the buildings to catch your breath. The wind would blow the snow so high against the barracks that it was very hard to open the door due to the high snow drifts blocking the door. I called this base, "the Siberia of the west."

There was a creek stretched across this base and it seemed as if all of the major facilities, such as the theater, post exchange, etc., were located across the creek. When a new airman would arrive on the base and ask, "Where is the post exchange," we would reply with a smile, "Across the creek." It seemed as though regardless of what anyone would ask for it was across the creek.

We were assigned to some barracks that looked like some of the barracks General Custer's men utilized during their fighting against the Indians. In fact, many of the airmen were saying that there were some barracks that still had signs up on the wall that stated, "You can take your squaws to your rooms, but there will be a heavy fine for shooting at buffalos out of the window." During the periods we were not attending communication classes, some of the airmen were assigned to keep the heat going in the barracks. Other airmen were assigned to work in the supply room or do other duties on the base. I remember being assigned to work in the supply room one day to put some supply packages together.

This white staff sergeant in charge of the supply room started a conversation about the Civil War between the North and the South. He was so emotionally involved with telling his story about how the Yankees soldiers killed women and children during that war that he would cry aloud. I would ask myself, *How in the hell did I happen to get picked to work with this Southern rebel.*

We would march in formation to communication classes during the early weeks of attending. It was so cold and windy that when we reached the class room it seemed as though all had tears coming out of their eyes. It is almost unexplainable how windy and cold it gets in the winter time on that base. Our class instructor notified the class that we should be prepared to get a test at the end of the week, and only the airmen who could type 30 words per minute would be attending day classes and the others would be attending night classes. This announcement sent chills through every airman's body because we knew that the weather was extremely cold and windy during the night period.

On the night prior to the test, I actually prayed and asked God to please help me pass that test. I had experienced the basics of typing while I was stationed in Korea, but I never considered myself a good typist. I was what you would call a good hunt and peck typist. I noticed that some of the airman on the teletype-writers seemed pretty fast during the warm-ups prior to the test. This really gave me something to think about. The instructor finally gave the word to begin the test and all I could think about was the cold and windy weather outside the building. When the instructor finally gave the word to stop the test, my heart was beating like an alarm clock. When the results of the test were being announced, you could hear a pin drop. When my name was called with a score of 41 words per minute, I said, "Thank you, Jesus." I was assigned to straight day shifts.

During the final week of our communication class, we were marching in formation past the reviewing stand in front of several officers. As we neared the stand, we received orders to give an eyes right as we were marching past the stand. All of a sudden, a strong wind started to blow so hard, it blew the chairs off of the reviewing stand and we were unable to stay in formation. The wind was blowing so hard, it seemed as if we were in the middle of a tornado. The reviewing officer stood up, grabbed the microphone, and hollered, "Run for cover." Some of us were able to run into some of the buildings and others took refuge behind the buildings that blocked the strong winds. However, no one was injured.

There were many hardships experienced by airmen stationed on this base. During the winter months, it would get so cold that different airmen were assigned as fire guards for the barracks to keep the fires burning continuously. They were responsible for the upkeep of heat in the barracks. That meant keeping the coal burning in the stove. If you were assigned as one of the fire guards and you let the fire go out because you fell asleep or other negligence, you were told that you could receive a court martial. There were instances when some airmen actually fell asleep during their tour of duty, but I did not stay around long enough to see the results.

The city of Cheyenne, Wyoming, where black and white airmen would visit during their off duty time was quite dull, at least for me as a black airman. There were approximately three establishments that black airmen patronized during my stay in the city. There was a lunch room run by a black woman where most of the prostitutes were available for propositions. The traffic in the lunch room consisted of mostly black airmen, but there was a trickle of white military men and civilians who stopped by to do trade with some of the black prostitutes. There was another bar on the other side of town that was frequented by black airmen, which was very cozy and clean. Many of us enjoyed visiting this bar because it had class. And then there was the American Legion club; the prices were supposed to be cheap, but it was very gloomy inside. Many of the black airmen frequented these establishments because of the security with the number of blacks in these clubs. There were other bars that some blacks patronized, but it was at their own risk. There were many stories of blacks entering bars run by whites and ending up being outnumbered and assaulted by racist whites.

It was always curious to me as to why whites could visit black establishments and very seldom blacks would bother them, but blacks had to always be on guard when they visited white establishments. The only instances where blacks would attack whites was when a drunken white would enter a black establishment drunk and start running off at the mouth with words like, "Nigger or Boy." Those were two words that could get a white man killed or send him to the hospital in serious condition. I was very happy to leave Cheyenne, Wyoming, because an outspoken black man could get into some serious trouble in this city.

I finally received my orders after completion of communications school assigning me to a base in Germany.

After spending a thirty-day furlough at home in Washington, D.C., I reported to Brooklyn, New York, to board a ship scheduled to leave for Germany.

Four

Germany; Tierra Amarilla, New Mexico; Winslow, Arizona

Germany

After we left Brooklyn, New York, by ship, we arrived in Bremerhaven, Germany, ten days later. During our first orientation after arriving in Germany, we were told by the chaplain that there were two things we should be careful about during our tour of duty in Germany. One was the German beer because it was much stronger than the American beer, and the other was to be very careful about the prostitutes because of venereal diseases that were out of control over there. Our destination when we departed from Bremerhaven was Wiesbaden, Germany. Our spokesperson said the train would be stopping in Frankfurt and the prostitutes would be walking around the station in columns of twos. When the train stopped in Frankfurt for a few hours, it seemed as though everyone vacated the train. We finally got everyone back on the train and arrived at our destination.

I was stationed on a base named Camp Lindsey in Wiesbaden, and black and white airmen lived in the same barracks. After duty hours we went our separate ways by choice. I had many white friends on the base, but frankly speaking, after confrontations with some of the prejudiced white commissioned and non-commissioned officers during duty hours on the base, it really turned you off against most whites. I was also a realist and I knew that most whites did not appreciate or want black airmen associating with those white German women. Although the whites knew there was nothing they could do to stop mingling between black airmen and German women, there were instances when white military police made a point of stopping you and harassing you if you were seen with a German woman at night.

German women were more likely to be stopped and questioned and asked for a pass if they were in the company of a black airman more often than in the company of white airmen. There were also many German people who looked down on German women associated with black airmen. German women associating with white airmen in certain bars considered themselves better than the German women associating with black airmen in bars. It was really a crazy world. But through all of these problems and confrontations, nothing could keep German women from socializing with black airmen.

There was one thing that bothered me deeply about the attitude of some Germans and that was the very thought that my father had fought against the Germans in World War I to defend freedom, and many of his buddies had died for the cause of freedom and many black soldiers died fighting the Germans to defend freedom during World War II. Now when I entered a German bar or store, they acted as though they did not want to serve or wait on me. I must say that most of that attitude came from racism that follows many white military men overseas. There are many Southern and some Northern white men who continue to believe that those Southern traditions will prevail. I am sorry to say that those individuals are in for a shocking awakening. There are many nationalities who observe how some whites try to treat us and they feel as though they can do the same. This is a very dangerous thought because serious harm could come to some people who believe that black men will not strike back if pushed to the limit.

Socializing on the base was the same as it had been on most bases with black and white airmen. In the clubs and day rooms, blacks would be mingling with their own and the whites would be with their own. During duty hours there was a difference because of the way we were assigned to certain positions; blacks and whites worked side by side.

One of the most noticeable violations I experienced during my tour of duty on that base, in fact on most bases, was the assignment of black airmen for duty during weekends and holidays. It seemed as though, regardless of how small the percentage of blacks were on any given base, there was always a larger percentage assigned on shift duty during Saturday, Sunday, Christmas, Memorial Day, Fourth of July, Thanksgiving, and New Year's Eve. In fact any time there was time off to be had, the blacks got the short end of the stick. I remember at various times Charge of Quarters (CQ) duty for me always fell on a Saturday or Sunday. I questioned the first sergeant as to why was this always happening to me. He advised me that he would look into it, and after he said that, I never received anymore CQ on weekends or holidays.

After spending approximately nine months in Wiesbaden, I was finally transferred to an Army base on the outskirts of Kaiserslautern, Germany. The name of the town was Vogel Way. There were two Air Force groups stationed on this all-Army base. Many of us were very pleased to be stationed on this base because there were many black Army soldiers stationed here. During this period, the Air Force was getting paid twice a month and the Army troops were only being paid once a month. During the middle of the month when some of our black brothers ran out of money, the black flyboys, as the Army soldiers would call us, would come their rescue in the form of buying drinks and sharing or lending them funds until their payday. When the first of the month came, those same soldiers would not let us flyboys buy anything. Everything would be on them. We were a very cohesive group of military men regardless of the different branches of service.

The city of Kaiserslautern was called "the sin city" because of the prostitutes, black marketing, alcohol, and many single women. There were bars and lunch rooms that mostly blacks frequented, and there were bars and lunch rooms that mostly whites frequented. There was also one big ballroom called the Atlantic Bar where Blacks and whites with their female companions would go and coexist after the smaller bars had closed. There were some racial incidents that happened in this ballroom, but most were due to action by intoxicated whites.

One night, four of us black airmen were riding

through a small town located about five miles outside of Kaiserslautern. We decided to stop at this German café to get a few beers. As we got out of the car to approach the café, we could hear the loud music playing on the accordion and the place was jumping. When we entered the door, the music stopped playing, and the people stopped dancing and began to walk back to their tables. I glanced around the establishment and did not see a black face in sight. I could feel the tension in the air, and it gave me a feeling of you are just not welcomed here.

I asked the German lady at the bar if we could get four beers. She replied that she would be unable to serve us. I asked her why and she said that it was not she who did not want to serve us, it was the demand of the white soldiers who were sitting at the table. I told her that we were not leaving until we had been served like everyone else in the bar. She stated that she was going to call the military police. I told her to call them because we were not going to leave until after we were served.

She proceeded to call the military police over the telephone. The military police asked to speak with me over the phone. He asked me what was the problem. I informed him that we had entered the bar and ordered four beers and were told that we could not be served. He asked to speak with the German lady. He asked her if we were starting any trouble. She replied that we were not. She was told that she would have to serve us as long as we were not causing any disturbance in the café. After that conversation, we were allowed to order four beers. We drank the beers, talked for about thirty minutes, and departed the bar.

I was involved in another incident in Kaiserslautern that almost caused a riot between black and white soldiers. I was visiting a nice little German bar with two German females and a friend of mine. As we entered the bar, I noticed that there were mostly white soldiers and a few German men. We ordered a round of drinks after we sat down and we decided to get up and dance to the music while we were waiting for our drinks. When we moved to the dance floor to dance, all of the people who were dancing on the floor stopped dancing and wandered back to their tables to sit down. This action left just my friend and me and the two German females on the floor alone. I really did not pay too much attention to the people leaving the floor until I heard a loud heavy voice coming from the back of the bar saying "What in the hell are those niggers doing in here?"

I was shocked and angry when I heard this voice, but I believe I was more angry than shocked. I asked my friend if he heard what I just heard. He said he did not hear anything. The German girl who was with my friend said she heard what he said and further stated that this was the same white soldier who had insulted her before. I really got angry then and I told my friend that I was going to the back of the bar and say something to this guy. He told me to forget it because we were outnumbered by white soldiers in the bar and there were no black soldiers in sight. I rushed back to the bar where the white soldier was sitting who made the remark and he leaned over on the bar, pretending that he had passed out from too much alcohol.

One of the white soldiers standing next to him whispered to me that he did not feel the same way as the guy who made the remark. At this moment, there was no reasoning in me. I told the white soldier lying on the bar that I was tired of receiving racial remarks and if he made those remarks because he thought we were outnumbered, I wanted him to wait there and I would return with some reinforcements. I departed that bar and went to a bar usually filled with black soldiers.

When I arrived at this next bar, I saw one of my army buddies and told him a white soldier had called me the magic word (Nigger). We were outnumbered by white soldiers and we needed some help. The word was passed around in the bar that we were going hunting. When we left the bar, there were approximately thirty black soldiers following me back to the bar where the incident happened. When we reached that German bar with sticks and bottles, the white soldiers and the German people were jumping out the windows and running out the back doors, trying to get away. The military police pulled up and prevented what could have been a full-fledged riot. There were other incidents in which black soldiers would enter bars with German women and were confronted by white Southern red necks. It was very seldom that you would see any friction when white soldiers would enter a bar where the majority in attendance were black unless a Southern white would get intoxicated and start calling black soldiers out of their name.

Tierra Amarilla, New Mexico

My three-year tour of duty ended in Germany and I received my military orders to report to a small Air Force station located in Tierra Amarilla, New Mexico. I received a thirty-day leave at home, and, prior to my departing for this site, I asked several people about the exact location of this base, but no one seemed to know where this base was. Some people said that there was probably a mistake on my orders because the only Amarilla they had heard of was Tierra Amarilla, Texas, but they never heard of a city like that in New Mexico.

After I finished my leave at home, I took my chances and headed for New Mexico. It never crossed my mind that I should have checked with one of the military bases in the Washington, D.C. area for information on that base. I believe it was partially because I had waited up until the last minute before I departed, was the reason for this oversight.

After boarding the train at the Union Station in Washington, D.C., we finally arrived in the state of New Mexico. I showed the conductor my ticket and asked him where would I be getting off. He told me that I would be getting off in Santa Fe, New Mexico, but he did not know how I would get to Tierra Amarilla. I noticed some Indians on the train selling beads and other items associated with the Indian nation. I believe they were authorized to sell those trinkets on the train to boost the tourist trade. One of the passengers said I should ask the old Indian Chief where Tierra Amarilla was located because he seemed to know a lot about the geographic locations in the state of New Mexico. I approached the chief and asked him how would I get to Tierra Amarilla, and he told me that it was located over a hundred miles north of Santa Fe. He also said he believed that I would have to catch a bus after I arrived there.

After arriving in Santa Fe, I asked one of the local residents where would I go to catch the bus going to Tierra Amarilla, New Mexico. He told me that I would have to walk a few blocks to the bus station, but the bus had left for that day and the next bus would not leave until eight-thirty A.M. the next day. This was very bad news for me because my military orders were only good until twelve o'clock midnight. I put my heavy duffel bag on my shoulder and started hitchhiking.

After walking for a while, I stopped and waited on the side of the road for about two hours before I finally got a ride. The driver told me that he would take me as far as he was going toward Tierra Amarilla, but he then would be turning off on another road not going my way. He stopped and let me off near a café located near a junction en route to the base. I thanked him and he left.

I stood by the roadside for about one hour, and I did not see one vehicle pass that way. I was getting a little concerned now because it was getting dark and I did not feel safe. So I decided to walk across the road to the café. The reasons why I did not go to the café at first were that (1) I believed that I would have gotten a ride by then and (2) I realized that I was in hostile territory after seeing all of those white people wearing cowboy boots and big straw hats. In fact I just did not want any trouble. It was getting late and time was running out. I did not have any other choice but to check the café out.

When I entered this little dingy café, there were two white patrons and a bartender who was also white. They were all in a deep conversation until I walked into the café, and, after seeing me, they stopped talking and everything got quiet. I spoke up and asked, "How far am I from the Air Force Station in Tierra Amarilla?" The bartender said, "Boy, you got a long way to go." I asked him if I could use the telephone to call the base. He pointed to the telephone located on the side of the café. I contacted the base and informed them that I was due to report to the base by twelve midnight, but it would be almost impossible for me to make it by that time due to transportation problems. They asked where was I located. I gave them the location, and they advised me to wait there and someone from the base would come and pick me up. While waiting for my transportation, I happened to glance up at a picture hanging on the wall. This painting was about six-by-six, showing about six to eight black men playing poker at a big table. It showed some of those men dressed up in partial tuxedos with no ties on, black derby-type hats on. They did not have any shoes on and aces and kings playing cards were sticking in between their toes.

After viewing this painting, it made me angry, but I considered the source. This incident only reminded me of some of the homes owned by Southern whites that had those little black jockeys posted outside of their residences. I walked outside of the café and waited until the Air Force vehicle came to pick me up. On my long ride back to the base, I could not stop thinking, *Here I am a*

United States military man putting my life on the line to defend people in this country like those in the café, and this is the type of reception I receive after returning back to the States.

It was late at night when we arrived at the Air Force station in Tierra Amarilla, New Mexico. I observed that this base was located far back in the woods and mountains. The next day after clearing onto the base, it was noted that there were approximately twenty black airmen out of a total of one hundred and thirteen airmen overall. This included officers too. A technical sergeant was the highest-ranking black airman on this small station, and I was the second highest ranking black airman on the station. We eventually got a black lieutenant assigned to the station.

The scene was the same as it was on most United States bases, with whites in complete control. If you smiled, grinned all the time, and laughed at their corny jokes, you were a good black boy. If you stood up for your rights and took your job seriously, you were considered to be a militant black wanting to create problems.

The weather in this area was very hot in the summertime and frigid in the winter. It was so cold on this base during one winter that there was an article in the paper stating that our K-9 dogs that patrolled the base got so cold they were wearing specially made shoes to protect their feet.

There were two towns not too far from the base that airmen visited. One was the town of Tierra Amarilla, which was located approximately three miles from the station. The other town was Chama, New Mexico, which was approximately eleven miles from the station. The town of Tierra Amarilla was a small town with nothing exciting going on, and most of the black airmen did not like to go there because many of the Spanish people made them feel uncomfortable. Some would act as though they did not want to be bothered with you, and if they did, it was only because you would spend money in town. The population was made up of mostly Spanish-Americans. Spanish girls living in Tierra Amarilla socializing with black airmen on the base were looked down on by the residents of the town. This was one town and one part of America where black airmen had to stick together in order to survive. In the town of Chama, the population was made up mostly of Spanish-American, a few blacks, and American Indians. During each year, some blacks would migrate from the State of Louisiana to cut trees in that area.

The majority of the Spanish-American community did not socialize with black airmen. There were few cases in which black airmen would have Spanish-American girlfriends. These same girls would be shunned by some of their own people and the white airmen. Many of the black airmen would wait for two or three months and drive to Albuquerque where there was a sizable black population to have a good time. This drive was over one hundred miles away.

One Saturday night, my friend Jackson and I decided to go to the town of Chama for a night out in the town. One of the white airmen said he was going to a little town on the other side of Chama, and he would gladly drop us off and pick us back up around 1:00 A.M. at the bar where he dropped us off. We left the base around ten-thirty that night and arrived in Chama around 11:00 P.M. Jackson was a very good softball player and he was well known throughout the Air Force stations in that area. While I was in the process of finding an empty booth in the bar to sit down, Jackson noticed some of his white friends from Los Alamos sitting in a booth located across the dance floor on the other side of the bar. He told me to secure the booth while he went over to talk to his friends. I ordered two beers while Jackson was holding a conversation with his friends. I noticed that the white female in the party started dancing with Jackson on the dance floor.

I glanced over to my right and I noticed a white man approaching the booth I was sitting in. He asked me to move over and I did because I thought that maybe he just wanted to ask me a question. After he sat down in the booth, he leaned over and whispered to me, "Nigger, you and your friend will have to leave this bar." I didn't want to believe what I was hearing, so I asked him why did he want my friend and me to leave the bar. He said, "Nigger, where I come from, niggers and white folks don't socialize in the same places." I asked him where did he come from. He said he was from Louisiana.

I told him in a quiet way that I was a military man and I eat sleep and work with white people every day and besides, I was not from Louisiana. I believe I stunned him by what I said because he had mistaken us for some of the black migrant workers who were working in that town because we were wearing civilian clothes. He jumped up from the booth and said, "It's not me, mister, it is my friends sitting over there at the table." I told him to go and tell his friends that as long as the owner of the bar said it was okay for us to enter his place, we were not leaving.

As he was leaving my booth, I glanced over at the table where he was headed and saw about five tobacco-chewing red-necks wearing straw hats sitting at that table. I had a little feeling of insecurity after seeing them, but I did not show any signs of fear. Jackson came back to the booth several times, but I did not want to tell him what had happened, not just yet. The reason I did not tell him yet was that he was one of those heavy muscular guys and I did not know what he would do because he feared nothing.

It was around twelve-forty when the bar started closing up and the patrons began to leave. I figured I would wait in the bar, and by time the bar closed, my friend would be there to pick us up. Jackson was still talking to his white friends when they pulled the cord out from the juke box and the waitress said everyone would have to leave.

Jackson and I walked out of the bar together, and I still had not mentioned the problem I encountered in the bar. After getting outside and not seeing my friend who was supposed to pick us up, and noticing those six white men in a group waiting for us, I whispered to Jackson that I had something to tell him. He asked me in a loud voice, "What did I have to tell him?" I said to him in a very calm voice that he should be on the alert because, while he was dancing with that white female, one of those white men came over to the booth I was sitting in and told me we would have to leave the bar. I told Jackson in a cool calm way, thinking he would react accordingly.

"Well," he asked me in a calm manner, "which one of the white men asked you to leave the bar?" I pointed slightly with my hand and said it was the white guy standing in that group of white men—one that was not wearing a hat. There were about twenty to twenty-five white people standing in the vicinity of the lot and just the two of us blacks. Jackson calmly walked over to the white man whom I had pointed out and asked him in a loud voice, "Why did you tell my friend that he would have to leave the bar?" The white man pulled out a pistol and told Jackson to move back towards the wall of the bar.

At this moment, I walked toward the friends of the white man and asked them to tell their friend to take the pistol that was pointed at my friend and put it in his pocket. They told me that they were not going to tell him anything and commented that "Jim will kill him too." After hearing these remarks, I approached the man with pistol and asked him to take the pistol away from my friend. He said, "Nigger, you put your hands up and back up against the wall too." There was a feeling of fear and helplessness in this vast area of darkness as thoughts ran through my mind about the killing of Emmett Till, the black teenager who was killed in the state of Mississippi a few years back. This white man was holding a loaded pistol pointed directly at us with intent to kill or maim both of us.

I looked up and spotted the sheriff's white car with the red light flashing on top coming toward us. The white man with the gun started running towards the woods behind the cars parked on the lot. The white sheriff jumped out of the car and asked me what was happening. I pointed toward where the man was running with the gun and said, "That man was holding a gun on my friend and me with intent to kill."

The sheriff went swiftly after the suspect in the direction that I had pointed out. We waited in front of the bar for approximately fifteen minutes and the sheriff finally returned. He said, "I have the gun." I asked him where was the individual who had the gun? He told me, "Don't you worry about that, you just prepare to be in court on Monday morning." I said, "Officer, usually when a man is apprehended with a dangerous weapon, you get the man and the weapon." He told me to shut up and not to worry about it. The ride we were looking for to take us back to the base had not arrived yet.

In the meantime, a black sheriff drove up in his car and started to talk to Jackson and me. During that period, the white sheriff walked a short distance through the parked automobiles and he returned talking with the suspect. I asked the black sheriff if he would take me back to the base, I would pay him. I also told him what had happened and he told me to wait a while until he went over and talked to the white sheriff who was talking to the suspect. The black sheriff returned back to where we were standing about fifteen minutes later.

He said, "Why don't you fellows forget about that incident?" I looked at him as if he was stone crazy. I told him, "This man pointed a gun at the both of us with intent to kill and you expect me to forget it." I kind of expected him to say something like that because he could only lock up black people in that town, as the saying goes. I asked him again was he going to take us back to the base and he said, "Get into the car." He went back over to talk to the white sheriff, and then the sheriff got into his car with the suspect and drove off. The black sheriff got into his car and followed them. My mind began to play tricks on me. I wondered whether they were going to take us back in the woods and do something to us. He finally turned off on the road leading back to the base and I was relieved.

As soon as I arrived on base, I entered this incident on the charge of quarters (CQ) logs. I was advised by the officer on duty that we should be prepared to go to court on Monday morning.

On Monday morning bright and early, Jackson and I were in Class A uniforms to go to court. We got into a United States Air Force military vehicle driven by the commanding officer, and the base chaplain rode along for our trip to Chama to meet our court date. During the trip, the chaplain, who was an Air Force major, turned around in the front seat toward me, continually trying to tell me that I could not come into other people's towns and try to tell them how to run their town. He also mentioned that his great-grandfather had slaves and everyone had his place. I told him that I was not interested in how many slaves his great-grandfather had, and I was only interested in seeing that justice would be achieved.

After we rode approximately half a mile through Chama, we stopped at this little gas station. I thought we were stopping here to get gas, but the commanding officer and the chaplain got out and started walking towards the station. Jackson and I got out to follow. The manager of the station walked up to the station from out in the yard to greet us. He was wiping some grease off of his hands and after he finished, he opened the door so we could get in. Before I entered the door, I noticed a white man who looked like he was an auto mechanic working on a car also walking toward the station. As he got nearer to the station wiping his hands, I recognized him as the same individual who had pulled the gun on us Saturday night. We proceeded into the station. The manager of the gas station was Spanish and later I learned he was the Justice of the Peace and the white man who was being charged worked for him. I could not believe what I was witnessing. The manager and the defendant started moving boxes, crates, and tables around in this dirty station to set up the court room. The arresting sheriff arrived and the manager put his court books on the table, hit his gavel on the table, and said, "Court is in session and the court will come to order."

I was asked by the manager, who was now the judge, to state my case. I told the judge how the incident started in the bar and how the defendant pulled the gun on both of us. After I finished my testimony, the judge told me to stay seated. He then called the arresting sheriff. I expected the sheriff to present evidence concerning the case but, to my surprise, I found out that the sheriff was the defense attorney for the defendant. The sheriff asked me, "You said you had a gun drawn on you, is that correct?" I replied, yes it was. He then asked, "What was the size of the gun?" Before I could say anything, the judge interceded and said, "It has already been established that there was a gun," so I should disregard that question. Jackson was called to give his testimony and was questioned about the incident by the sheriff. After his testimony, the judge said he was calling for a recess.

We all left the gas station and went to get lunch at a café during the recess. When we entered the café, the judge, sheriff, and the defendant sat at one table. The commanding officer, chaplain, Jackson, and I sat at another table across the room. After approximately one hour, we all returned to the gas station. The judge hit his gavel on the table and called the court to order. He started off by saying that he believed that all men were created equal and there should be no discrimination anywhere. He said, however, he did not believe that he had the authority to render a decision in this case. He then said as far as he was concerned, the case was closed. The defendant walked up to the judge's table, picked up his gun and bullets, and walked out of the door. I was in a state of shock, I could not believe something like this could happen.

During the entire trip back to the base, there was nothing but silence in the car. The commanding officer or the chaplain did not mention a word about the results of the trial.

When we arrived back on the base and entered the barracks to change clothes, the black airmen wanted to know the outcome of the trial. I told some of the airmen what had happen and the word spread around the base. Many of the black airmen wanted to go to Chama that night to find those white men. I told them to forget it because it would only cause more trouble.

Somehow the word got back to the commanding officer that the black airmen were going to Chama that night and tear it up. The public address system was calling me loud and clear to report to the commanding officer immediately. I reported to the commanding officer and he asked me to have a seat.

He said, "Sergeant Gurley, I am going to put the town off limits this evening because I hear that the black troops are going to town and start some trouble tonight." He said, "I am going to call all of the black airmen together in the day room and I want you to tell them the reason the white man was found not guilty was because there was not enough evidence."

I told him, "Sir, I could not honestly live with myself if I told those airmen that lie." I asked him why had he called me to tell the black airmen about this incident. He said, "Sergeant Gurley, I remember another meeting we held and the black airmen nodded their heads in agreement with everything you said." I said to the commander that there was no way I could mislead the airmen. I saluted and departed from his office.

About twenty minutes after my leaving the commander's office, a runner went through each barrack notifying all black airmen including myself to report to the day room for an important meeting. After we were all seated in the day room, the chaplain was introduced to speak. He started off by saying, "We have called this emergency meeting because we do not want any serious trouble to start in town." He said the reason the man was not convicted at the trial held in Chama this morning was that there just wasn't enough evidence. At that very moment,

I stood up, walked forward to the front of the day room, and said, "Men, at first I was not going to speak on this incident, but the chaplain is lying to you and to me. I am saying that the reason the white man was not convicted this morning was that he was found innocent before the trial began." I said there was overwhelming evidence presented that he pulled a gun on Jackson and me with intent to kill, but it was not even taken under consideration. After I had finished my statement, the chaplain continued to tell his side of the story, but I believe no one was really paying attention to what he was saying.

About one week later, I was in my room that was located upstairs overtop of the mail room. The mail clerk entered my room and said he had some mail for me. He handed me two letters, but I noticed that one of them was addressed to my mother in Washington, D.C. I believe the mail clerk made a mistake when he took the mail to the post office. Some way that letter was left in his bag without being mailed out and he put the incoming mail back in the same bag. I believe that he saw Gurley on the letter and he assumed it was addressed to me. I opened the letter and the letter read,

> Dear Mrs. Gurley,
>
> Your son, Staff Sergeant George Gurley is stationed on this base. He is trying to pass his dislike about the base to influence some of the younger airmen on the base. If he continues to do this, he will no longer be a non-commissioned officer.

I did not want to get the mail clerk in trouble, so after

reading the letter, I tore it up and flushed it down the toilet. I did not want to overreact, but truthfully speaking, I had to think this one out.

I waited about three days and then I decided that I really needed some help before they began to build a case up on me and tried to get me thrown out of service. I discussed this situation with other black airmen and they agreed that I would have to do something. I started writing a letter to the Pentagon explaining what they were trying to do to me on the base. I wrote about the Chama incident, the letter that was sent to my mother and other bad conditions on the base. After finishing the letter, I sent it out special delivery.

Approximately two months later after sending the letter off, an Inspector General's (IG) team landed on this small airport outside of town and arrived on the base. After a day of investigation, later on in the week, I received a letter of apology from the commanding officer, personnel officer, and the first sergeant for sending that letter to my mother. There was nothing in the letter mentioned about the Chama incident.

About four weeks later, we got a new commanding officer and a new first sergeant. The first sergeant let it be known that it would not be business as usual on the base. He started out by putting a black airman in charge of the non-commission officers club and other blacks in charge of a few facilities located on the base.

Those new appointments by the new first sergeant, evidently infuriated some of the Southern white airmen because someone burned a cross directly beneath his sleeping quarters. The flames were extinguished before they could do any extensive damage. No one was apprehended or charged for this incident, but the message was clear that someone didn't approve of what he was doing with the replacement by black airmen. The first sergeant was from Arizona and he was a firm but fair white man. He made it clear that he had been sent in as a trouble shooter on the base and that there would be no racial incidents on his base. The new commander was a straight shooter also and concurred with whatever actions the first sergeant initiated.

Several weeks later, I was riding back to the base through town with Airman Smith around 10:00 P.M. on that particular night. Airman Smith had an upset stomach, and I advised him to stop at this café and I would order him a sandwich and a quart of milk to settle his stomach. I knew that this café was one of the hangouts for some of the white airmen on the base, but I never gave it a second thought after it was clear that my friend needed some help. This was my first time entering the café, but I went directly to the proprietor and told him I had a sick buddy out in the car and I would like to order two ham sandwiches and a quart of milk. He told me that I would have to wait in the back part of the kitchen while he fixed my sandwiches. I asked him why and he went into this long explanation about how he had to look out for his business and he would have trouble with his customers if I sat at one of the tables while waiting for my order. I told him to forget the order and left the premises.

I told my buddy what had transpired inside the café and told him I was going to report that incident when we returned to the base. He told me to forget it because that was the way those people were, but I was burning up with frustration. I told him that most of the business in town comes from the military men stationed here and we were all here to protect the skies for them and they don't even want to serve us because of the color of our skin. When we arrived on the base, I went straight to the first sergeant's room and woke him up to tell him about the incident. He told me that he would check that establishment out the next day.

Around 10:00 A.M. the next morning, the first sergeant paged for me to report to the orderly room. He asked me about the incident and then asked me what did I want him to do about it. He asked me did I want to make that establishment off limits for all military men on the base? I told him that I did not want to put it off limits for everyone, but, I did want the café to be available for all people regardless of race, creed, or color. I told him that if this was accomplished, then I would be satisfied. He told me that he was going talk with the commander and then they were going to ride down to the café and discuss this matter with the manager. He would contact me when he returned.

Approximately four hours later, the commander and the first sergeant returned to the base and I was paged to report to the orderly room. He said, "Sergeant Gurley, I want you and your friend to visit that same café again and let me know how you were treated." I thanked the first sergeant for his positive initiative and departed from the orderly room.

Later that evening Airman Smith and I departed from the base to find out whether the first sergeant was telling the truth about the change in policy at the café in town. When we arrived at the café, we entered and were greeted by the manager. He said, "Sergeant Gurley, the meal is on me this evening." He instructed the cook to fix two steak dinners. He apologized for the incident that had happened last night and said we were welcome to come to his café as often as we wanted to.

Shortly after the closures of several incidents while stationed on this base, I finally received orders transferring me to Winslow, Arizona.

Winslow, Arizona

Winslow, Arizona, was a small town with a population of a few thousand people, with a mixture of Indians, Spanish, whites, and a few black families. I felt a little more comfortable in this town because of the black families who were living there. Openly you could not detect racism in the town, but deep down within yourself you knew it was present. I experienced it dining out in white-owned and run cafés and you could sense that you were not wanted there. I vividly remember patronizing a black-owned café bar and the black American Legion club. There was intermingling with the Indians, whites, and Spanish people who frequented these black establishments. The Air Force station was located approximately ten miles outside of the town of Winslow. There was a total of one hundred and ten white airmen on the base, fifteen civilians, and about eight black airmen. There were no black officers, and I was the highest ranking noncommissioned officer, with the rank of Staff Sergeant.

The day I arrived on the base, I reported to the orderly room to meet the first sergeant. The first individual I met when I entered the orderly room was a white airman who had been stationed with me on the base I just left in New Mexico. After we greeted each other, he introduced me to the first sergeant. He told the sergeant, "This is Sergeant Gurley and you had better watch him because he will get your job." We all laughed because he said it in a joking way. He was really referring to the incident in Tierra Amarilla, New Mexico, when the first sergeant and the base commander were replaced. I really had the gut feeling that this sergeant was well aware of what had happened prior to my arriving at this station. I knew that this was just like another Air Force station in the network of bases located in this part of the country used for air defense. Mostly all of the base commanders and first sergeants knew one another by first name. It was just like one big happy family. If there was what you would call a problem with an individual in the family, someone would be in a position to get him.

I did not have to wait long before I found out that this first sergeant was out to get me. He assigned me to be barrack chief where I was living. He held a barracks inspection almost every week, and it seemed as though regardless of how hard we worked on our barracks to get them clean, he would always find something wrong with it. At first I did not pay too much attention to his actions although some of the airman kept telling me that he only held inspections after he was drinking. I began to check some of the other barracks after some of his inspections and after seeing the condition those barracks were in and passing inspection, I knew something was wrong. At times I would stay up with the airmen sometimes until three or four o'clock in the morning preparing the barracks for inspection. The first sergeant would still find something wrong. I knew then that I would have to cover my backside or, as the troops would say, "my ass."

One night I was scheduled to work a swing shift (four to twelve), on my regular job and the white sergeant who was my shift leader changed my shift because I had requested to attend an affair in town. The next day, the first sergeant called me into his office and told me he was going to court martial me. I asked him why and he told me that he had called over to where I was supposed to be working last night and I was not on duty. I told him that my shift leader had authorized me to be off last night. He told me that it did not make any difference what my shift leader authorized me to do because as far as he was concerned, I was scheduled to work the swing shift that night. I told him that he had better check with my shift leader before he began any court martial proceedings. After that conversation, I never heard anymore about a court martial.

The first sergeant was a chronic beer drinker. Every evening after he would leave the orderly room, he would go straight to his room and start drinking beer. On weekends he would go to some of the barracks and start drinking beer with his white buddies.

The harassment continued from the first sergeant. I would continue to use tact by telling him whenever he raised hell with me about the barracks inspection, that we would do better the next time. I knew this action really bugged him because he wanted me to break down and beg for mercy. Never within my wildest dreams would I give him the satisfaction of breaking me down. I also did not want him to charge me with insubordination, so I would be very careful in choosing every word I said to him. He had a habit of joking and playing with some of the lower ranked black airmen, but he was dead serious every time we confronted each other. Frankly speaking, I would not have wanted it any other way.

One Monday morning, we were all sitting in the dining hall eating breakfast when one of the black airmen asked me if I heard about what the first sergeant had said to one of the black airmen on Sunday. I told him no and asked him, "What did he say?" He told me that the first sergeant had called Airman Robinson a nigger. He also stated, "You know how the first sergeant is when he is drinking." I asked him what did Robinson do when he called him a nigger. He said Robinson just walked away from him. I asked the airman, "Where is Robinson now?" I was told that he was over in the barrack. I walked over to the barrack and confronted the airman with what was told to me. He said yes it was true, but he did not want to start any trouble. I explained to him, "The only way we are going to stop these racial incidents is to do something about them when they first start." I asked him that if I spoke to someone about this incident, would he back the story up? He agreed to do that and he also said that there were also other black airmen present who heard him also. This was all I wanted to hear.

I walked up to the orderly room and asked the first sergeant if I could speak with the commanding officer. He walked back into the commander's office and after a few minutes, he instructed me to enter. The commander told me to close the door and have a seat. He then asked me what was the problem. I told him that this was a small base with minorities stationed on it and the first sergeant should be capable of realizing the sensitivity involved with all personnel. I was told by one of the black airmen that the first sergeant had called him a nigger during one of his drinking sprees and if he was not removed as first sergeant of this base, I was going to contact the NAACP. He asked me where it happened and who was the black airman involved. I gave him the information he asked for and he told me he would contact me later.

On Wednesday morning, I was paged on the public announcement system to report to the commander's office. I reported as requested and he told me that the first sergeant was being reassigned to another base effective Friday of this week. He then asked me if I still wanted to contact the NAACP. I told him no because I was satisfied with the action.

He asked me if there were any other changes I would like to see made. I told him that there was one more request I would like to make. I told him that there was only one bar in town that black airmen patronized and that was still off limits. I asked him would he see that it was put back on limits. He smiled and told me to check back with him after he made a few phone calls. I talked to him later on that day and he said the bar was now back on limits. I thanked him and went to spread the word to the rest of the black airmen.

During the following weeks on the base, it was pretty quiet and everyone seemed relaxed and contented. We never received a replacement first sergeant, but we had an acting first sergeant who got along with everyone.

One Sunday night, I was sitting at a bar in the city of Winslow when I noticed this white man standing at the end of the bar. He stood out from the rest of the patrons because he was wearing cowboy boots and a great big white ten-gallon hat. It was obvious that he was one of the regular customers in the bar because he seemed to know the bartender and many of the other black civilians present in the bar. He was spending a lot of money buying drinks for some of the patrons and he seemed to be kinda tipsy. All of a sudden, he hollered out, "They should send all you niggers back to Africa." I looked at my two Air Force buddies and they looked back at me. There was also a black civilian present who was driving one of those big tractor trailer rigs passing through on his way to Texas. He asked me if I heard what the white man had just said. I told him, "I sure did and he really should not be in here." He said, "I am going to get him for saying that when he leaves out of here." I walked over to my two buddies and told them what the truck driver had said. I told them that we did not want to get into any trouble in this bar. The black civilians were laughing at what the white man had said, but it was not a bit funny to me or my buddies. Evidently the bartender had told this white man to leave because he figured that black airmen from the base were a little upset and there was going to be some trouble. The white man started toward the door, with the truck driver in hot pursuit behind him.

When he reached the sidewalk outside the bar, the truck driver and the white man started fighting. The driver swung at the white man, striking him up side the head. This was a huge white man and he weighed around two hundred and eighty pounds. When he received the blow on the head, he shook it off and grabbed the truck driver as if he were a little toy. My buddy Williams, who weighed around two hundred and seventy-five pounds and was about seven feet tall, saw that the truck driver was losing the fight. So he began to struggle with this white man. He hit this man so hard that it seemed as though he flipped in the air and landed on the street curb.

During this course of action, another white man walked up with a lunch bucket in his hand and said, "You boys leave that white man alone." This white man proceeded to grab Jones and they started fighting. Williams came over, grabbed this man, and hit him so hard he hit his head on the sidewalk and did not move. The truck driver told us to hurry up and get in the truck so he could drop us off at the base. When he pulled off in his truck, he wanted to run over the white man lying in the street. I told him not to do that because it seemed as though this white man was already in serious condition. When he pulled off, I grabbed the steering wheel to prevent the driver from almost running over the man. The truck driver drove us to the base and when we entered the base, I could not help but think about that white man who was lying on the highway. All of this would have never happened if this white man in the bar had kept his mouth shut.

The next morning while we were eating breakfast in the dining hall, one of the black airmen said, "I heard what you guys did to that white man in town." He said, "You guys killed that man." I really felt sick then because I did not know whether he was lying or telling the truth. After leaving the dining hall, I started walking towards the barracks and I heard an announcement over the public address system paging me to report to the orderly room. When I reached the orderly room, the clerk told me that I had a telephone call. I picked up the telephone and it was the town sheriff on the other end. He asked me if I was in town last night. I told him, "Yes, I was." He told me that he would like for me to come in town to his office as soon as possible because he wanted to talk to me. I contacted Airmen Williams and Smith, told them about the call I had received from the sheriff, and said we would have to let the commanding officer know what happened last night. We contacted the commander and he drove us down to the sheriff's office.

When we arrived at the sheriff's office, he had already interviewed some of the black civilians in town and all he wanted to know from us was who participated in this brawl. He had put out a police bulletin to stop the truck driver on the highway. The truck driver was escorted out of a jail cell for additional interrogation because he had told the sheriff that he did not know anything about the incident. Airman Williams asked the sheriff to leave him with the truck driver for about five minutes and he would get the truth out of him. Airman

Smith and I were locked up in a jail cell until Airman Williams talked with the truck driver.

While we were in the cell, the sheriff was talking with one of his deputies and said, "We don't have any trouble down here until we get some of those niggers down here from the North." This really made us realize that we were dealing with some red neck Southerners. The driver finally told the truth about the incident and we were let out of the cell to go back to the base. The sheriff told the commander that we would have to report for a court trial a week from this date. He also said one of the white men was still in the hospital with a concussion.

We reported to the court on the date scheduled at about 10:00 A.M. in the morning. It was a small room and neither one of the white men were present. The only people present were a white judge who looked to be about eighty years old, a prosecutor, the commanding officer, the truck driver, and the three airmen from the base. The prosecutor called Airman Williams to the stand first and questioned him extensively about the incident. When Airman Smith was called to the stand by the prosecutor, it really seemed as though he was giving him a rough time and it really did not look good for the defendants. They did not even have a defense attorney. Although I was not accused of any crime, after the prosecutor got through with Airman Smith, I asked the judge could I say something about the incident.

The judge said yes and requested me to come to the front and be sworn in. After the judge swore me in, I told the judge that at first I was not going to testify, but after hearing how the prosecutor was trying to put words in

Airman Smith's mouth, "I don't have any other choice but to put this incident in its right perspective." I said, "First of all, Your Honor, I do not believe that a black man would get a fair trial in the South." The judge looked at me hard and took his glasses off. He said, "Why do you believe that a black man would not get a fair trial in the South?" I told him, "One of the reasons that I believe that is because a white man pulled a gun on my friend and me in Chama, New Mexico, and although there was enough evidence to convict him for the crime, the court let him go free." The judge then asked me to tell him what happened at the café. I told him that the white man provoked the incident by calling African-Americans out of their name with the use of the word "nigger." I said this incident caused a chain of reaction that got several people involved in this unfortunate brawl. The judge called for a recess prior to rendering a decision.

The judge stayed out of the courtroom for about thirty minutes. He returned and called the court to order. He said, "It is really tragic when there are serious incidents such as this one." He said, "We are now confronted with the fact that we have one man in the hospital and one man hurt." The judge said different races were born to get along with each other on the face of the earth. He said although it was unfortunate that this incident happened, he was going to dismiss this case in favor of the defendants. The old judge looked up at me and whispered to me, "Do you still believe that a black man would not get a fair trial in the South?" I replied, "No sir." We departed from the court and returned to the base free men.

After the incident at Winslow, Arizona, I received my

military orders to report to Thule, Greenland. After taking a furlough at home for a few days, I reported to McGuire Air Force Base to catch my airplane flight to my destination.

Five

Thule, Greenland; Anchorage, Alaska; Homer, Alaska

Thule, Greenland

We departed from the base during the month of October 1959, and landed in Goose Bay, Labrador, before continuing on to Thule, Greenland. After spending a short time on this base, we departed for our lengthy trip to Thule. We were only airborne for approximately twenty minutes when I pulled the curtains back on the window to look out. I noticed some smoke pouring out of the right engine of the plane. I did not want to panic or cause any panic, and I also did not want to believe what I was seeing. I reached over the seat in front of me, gently touched this white sergeant on the shoulder, and quietly asked him to look out of the window and tell me whether he saw what I saw out of the window.

He quickly pulled the curtain back and when he looked back to tell me what he had seen, I noticed that he was looking kind of weird in the eyes. He tried to convince me that it was only vapors in the sky due to the high altitude of the plane. His wishful thinking subsided pretty fast when the "no smoking" sign and "fasten your seatbelt" light came on. The pilot's smooth voice came over the intercom system saying, "We are experiencing some problems and we will be returning to Goose Bay for a landing." We finally landed with no injuries involved, but it scared the hell out of everyone on the plane.

We waited patiently in the air terminal until the mechanics looked over the plane. We were told later that the reason for the smoke coming out of the engine was that the air vent on the engine was stuck and would not open, causing the engine to overheat. It was also mentioned that most of the fuel had to be dispersed prior to our landing to prevent a possible explosion. While we were waiting for the plane to be checked over, I wondered why another plane was not used to fly us to Thule, but we were reminded that we would be flying in that same plane after it got fixed. We finally departed but my heart was in my mouth during the entire lengthy flight to Thule.

After landing, we departed the plane and took that long walk to the air terminal. The military personnel whom we were replacing were so glad to see us because they were finally going to be released from this ice box. The weather was just beginning to get extremely cold.

I often wondered if my encounters with the first sergeants in Tierra Amarillo, New Mexico and Arizona, were the reason I received this frigid assignment.

Race relations between black and white airmen on Thule, Greenland, were fair, and I believe that this was due to the isolation and very little contact with the outside world. There was a saying in Thule that, "After you stay in Thule for at least four months, you get what you call the 'Thule-ight-tus.' " This was considered the length of time after which everyone gets mad at everything and wants to fight. During this period, one has to be careful of what you say to anyone. This was also a period when you would look at someone wearing a parka during the dark season with a truck light shining on that person, it looked like a woman with long hair.

Although there were some black and white airmen who socialized with one another, for the most part, we kept mostly to ourselves. My guess was that when most whites started drinking or got drunk, most of them did not know what to say out of their mouths. So if you wanted to keep out of trouble, you did not socialize with them.

After spending approximately four months in Thule, I received a telegram in the orderly room stating that my mother was seriously ill at Andrews Air Force Base Hospital and was not expected to live until the next day. I received the telegram after the first sergeant called me into his office to give it to me. He displayed no sympathy at all. In fact, he had the nerve to ask me if I really wanted to go home. I told him, hell yes, I wanted to go home and I wanted the first thing smoking leaving out of Thule. I went to visit the Red Cross to seek some assistance, and the Red Cross worker tried to convince me that there was nothing I could do by going home. I almost went berserk. I proceeded to ask him whether he would want to go home if his mother were in the hospital on her dying bed. Only then did he begin to process my papers to go home.

I departed Thule, Greenland, on that same day and arrived in Washington, D.C., the next day. I was given a fifteen-day furlough to straighten out my business. After visiting my mother at Andrews Air Force Base Hospital, she responded to my visit immediately. Even the doctors told me that I was the best medicine for her. Two days prior to my scheduled departure back to Thule, my mother began to get very ill. I contacted the personnel office at the Pentagon and requested to be stationed at a base close to home so I could be near to my mother while she was still recuperating in the hospital. I was informed by one of the officers at the Pentagon that they would not be able to honor my request. I then requested to meet with someone in the Pentagon whom I would be able to explain my situation to in person. I was granted an appointment scheduled for the next day.

I met with an Air Force officer the next day at the Pentagon. He listened very careful to my situation and my request. He then told me that it would be almost impossible for me to get a transfer from Thule, Greenland, regardless of how serious the problem was. He said if he would transfer me, everybody in Thule would want a transfer. I mentioned to the officer that I appreciated his giving me the opportunity to speak about my problem, but if he could not help me in any way, I would like to speak with one of the Joint Chiefs of Staff. He immediately told me that I did not have to do that. He said, "You call me at this telephone number around this same time tomorrow." He would let me know something.

I called the next day and was told that orders were being cut to reassign me to Andrews Air Force Base until my mother recovered. My mother passed away three months later.

Anchorage, Alaska

Eight months later, I received my military orders assigning me to Elmendorf Air Force Base located near Anchorage, Alaska.

The city of Anchorage had a large population and there was a mixture of Eskimos, whites, and a few blacks living there. This was my first observation of how some Eskimos live in Alaska. I had been told that conditions of Eskimos were horrible in Alaska. From what I observed, some of these people were living in worse poverty areas than many blacks in the lower states in America. I also noticed that blacks tended to socialize mostly with their own and whites did the same. Although there was some socializing between the races in some of the main clubs in Anchorage, it was not to a great degree.

I was stationed on Elmendorf Air Force Base for approximately six to eight months, waiting for my top secret security clearance. During that period, I was not allowed to work in any restricted areas on the base. You were also issued a different identification badge that made you stand out from airmen wearing the secured badges. This made you feel like an outcast because airmen wearing the secured badges would keep their distance from you.

I was assigned to work in the mail room during this period, and I was not allowed to wander anywhere else in the building. I felt honored to be assigned to this squadron because everyone was highly motivated and intelligent. I just wanted the investigators to hurry up and complete my security clearance.

After being confined to working in that certain area

for so many days without receiving my security clearance, I requested to be assigned to one of the Air Force sites on the Aleutian chain. Now there were many stories about some of those sites and some of them were not too comforting. Some of the stories spoke about the wind blowing so hard on some of those Islands during the winter months that if you did not tie yourself down you would be blown out into the Bering Sea.

Homer, Alaska

I was finally granted my request to be transferred to one of the sites. When I reported to the administration building located on the base (called the Kremlin because it resembled the one in Moscow) to be processed, I knew the sergeant processing the transfers. He asked me where would I like to be assigned on the Aleutian chains. I told him I was not too enthusiastic about going to any one of them, but if I was going, I would like to be sent to one that was not too far out in the boondocks. He said, "Sergeant Gurley, I am going to send you to a site located in a place called Homer, Alaska." He said this site was called the Bermuda of the Aleutian chains. He said that not because of the warmth of the town but because it was located near a town with people living nearby. I thanked him for his assistance, and I was well on my way to Homer, Alaska.

I boarded one of those small planes to reach Homer, Alaska, and with flying in between the clouds and the mountains on the way there, I was one happy soul when we finally landed. I boarded a military vehicle and proceeded on this road that went up and around this mountain until we reached the top. It was a beautiful view from atop the mountain, but the weather was ferocious.

This was a small site but had a mini post exchange, bar, dining hall, and everything needed to keep one comfortable. We could go outside and learn how to ski during our off-duty time. Some of the airmen would try out the skis without an instructor and wind up running into a tree at the bottom of the hill.

We had to be careful outside during the bear season because they would chase you if you crossed their paths. I remember one day during the spring season some of us were sitting in the club and due to the heat, the bartender opened the side door to let some air in. While some of us were dozing and some of us were drinking beer and just talking about memories of home, a great big black bear stuck his head in the side door. We finally got him to leave, but you could see nothing but skid marks on the floor where many of us struggled to get out of that area. We never left that door open again.

Once in a while, some of the airmen would ride down into the town, but most of our time was spent on the base.

I received my military orders assigning me to Andrews Air Force Base in the State of Maryland. I was very happy to be returning to a base close to my home in Washington, D.C. My main concern was what type of white officers and non-commission officers I would be working for when I reported for duty. The question was would most of them be from the North or the South? *I must remember to always cover my ass regardless of what I do.* This was beginning to be a routine thought with me after experiencing so many confrontations with Southern whites in the military.

I was surprised when I reported to my squadron because I was greeted by a black first sergeant. I must admit that at times, some black officers and non-commission officers can be as bad as and sometimes worse than the whites. Many of them feel as though they have to prove something to whites and they look to make an example out of some unsuspecting black.

There was this white chief master sergeant stationed in the squadron, and we used to call him "the great white father." He was known for his drinking exploits, and he was well known on the base and in some of the bars off base. He was the chief in the section where I worked. If you were one of the good ole boys or one of his drinking partners, you were all right, but if you crossed his path otherwise, you were in trouble.

The work in my section during this period was more mentally than physical stressing. We were working thirty straight days, thirty straight swing shifts, and thirty straight midnight shifts with very little rest. One of the reasons we were working so hard, so we were told, was that one of the systems had broken down and caused a big backlog of traffic.

On one of the midnight shifts, I was working as supervisor of the aisle and there was a security violation committed. On that particular night, I observed a white airman working on one of the machines, but I did not pay too much attention to him because they did it all the time. The next morning, after getting off duty and returning to the barracks, I was notified that someone wanted to speak with me back in my section.

When I reported back to the section, I was called back in a room where the colonel, chief master sergeant, and the flight sergeant were waiting for me. The colonel told me that there had been a security violation on my shift the previous night and due to the fact that I was the aisle supervisor, I would have to accept the blame. I explained to them that they should check the white airman who was working on the equipment during the time of the incident. This white colonel with his Southern drawl said, "Sergeant Gurley, you can't expect me to put the blame on someone else when you were the supervisor."

I told him that there had been numerous complaints from other supervisors about maintenance working on the equipment without proper supervision but the practice still continued. I explained to him that the maintenance men were supposed to report to the aisle supervisor before working on any equipment and he proceeded to work on the equipment without notifying me. I was not going to accept any blame for that incident. I was ordered to leave the center and they would talk to me later.

I was called into the center the next day by the same little crew, and they went through the same routine, trying to put the blame on me. I now realized that they were getting pretty serious about putting the blame on me for this incident. It was quite obvious that they were trying to frame me for something I did not do.

The next day around noon, I got in my car and drove downtown in Washington, D.C. to the NAACP office. I spoke with Mr. Clarence Mitchell, who was the director of the agency at that time. I explained to him that I was having some problems on Andrews Air Force Base. He asked me what was the problem. I told him that they were trying to frame me on the base for something I was not guilty of, although I explained to them who the guilty party was. He asked me who was the first sergeant. I told him that he was a black sergeant. He asked me if he was an Uncle Tom? I told him I really didn't know at this time. He said, "Let me call the base first."

Mr. Mitchell picked up the phone, contacted the base, and asked to speak with the first sergeant. He told the first sergeant that one of his men was in his office complaining about unfair treatment on the base and if it continued, he would have to investigate. The sergeant told Mr. Mitchell to put me on the phone. He asked me to report back to the orderly room where we could discuss the problem. Mr. Mitchell told me to go back to the base and talk to him, but if there were any further problems to contact him as soon as possible. I thanked him for his assistance and left his office.

I reported back to the first sergeant in the orderly room to explain to him what had happened. Evidently the sergeant had contacted the colonel because I was ordered to report to see him over at the work center.

When I reported to the colonel, he was smiling and told me to have a seat. He said, "Sergeant Gurley, I want you to forget all about that incident. In fact, you can consider that case closed." I was a little apprehensive when he said that, but I was also glad it was over. My first thoughts were, *What's in store for me now?*

I did not have to wait long to find out what was in

store for me because within a few weeks, I received orders assigning me to the First Mobile Squadron located on Clarke Air Force Base in the Philippine Islands.

Six

Philippine Islands, Vietnam, Thailand

Philippine Islands

I arrived in the Philippine Islands during the month of May 1964. I remember this period very vividly because a week prior to my arrival, a plane had crashed at Clark Air Base during landing and the skeleton of the burned-out plane was still visible near the air terminal. I was told by some airmen stationed on Clark Air Force Base at that time that some of the military personnel that were killed on that flight were bowlers returning from a tournament that was held in Hawaii. They said their families were waiting in the airport for their arrival when it happened.

I was just getting used to the Philippines and having a great time until I was called to the orderly room one day in July and told that orders had been cut sending me to Vietnam to replace an airman who was returning to this base. I did not panic, but I was not too enthusiastic about going either. This feeling was due to the many conversations I had heard from Vietnam veterans returning from over there. I was living in a barracks where airmen returning from Vietnam would stay in when they returned.

You could tell when they checked in because it was usually all hours of the night when they returned. They would check in late at night, wearing those go-to-hell hats (a Vietnam soldiers' trademark) cocked on the side of the head, the lights would be switched on, they would kick the footlockers, and there would be loud talking. There was no one in the barracks who had the nerve or guts to challenge them. We were a little apprehensive because we thought they were combat crazy.

We boarded a plane headed for Vietnam. When we were going in for a landing at Tan Son Nhut Air Force Base located outside of Saigon, I looked out of the window of the plane and from my view, I could see green trees and the beautiful landscape of the country. It looked so peaceful that no one would have believed that there was a war going on.

When we landed and got off of the plane, reality set in because I asked one of the airmen what those boxes were waiting to be loaded on the plane. I was told that they were some boxes containing military men killed in action being loaded on a plane for shipment back to the States. I began to look at the situation from a more serious perspective.

I never realized that the base I was supposed to report to in Vietnam was so far north of Saigon. I was going to a town by the name of Quang Nai. I asked almost every soldier I approached, where was this town located. It seemed as though no one I asked knew where it was. The atmosphere on this base was one similar to being in a large train station. Everyone was walking at a fast pace, as if going around in circles. There were Special Forces

Soldiers and other soldiers and airmen walking around with knives and pistols strapped around their legs. Some South Vietnamese people and their families were waiting to board one of the American military planes with cattle. Most of their belongings were on their heads and backs. I could not believe what I was seeing.

I walked over to where this white army soldier was sitting beside a wall and asked him if he knew where Quang Nai was. He said he was stationed there. He came down to pick up supplies and he was waiting for his plane to leave. I told him that I would follow him when he boarded his plane going north. I remembered that the weapon I received prior to leaving the Philippines was issued to me without any ammunition. I was advised at that time that I would receive it when I arrived at my destination. I was not too bothered about not having any ammunition at this time because it was very peaceful and I could not hear any gun fire.

Prior to our boarding the plane, the flight chief who would be on the plane gave us instructions on what we should do in case of an emergency situation on the plane. He said when we heard one buzzing signal, that would be an alert and the signals following that buzzing meant that there was immediate danger. After he finished with his presentation, I walked around the plane to check it out before we began the flight. What I really observed, after looking at the plane, did not make me feel any better. First of all it looked as if oil was smeared over the side windows and the engines looked as though they had recently caught fire. When we boarded the plane for takeoff, my first order of business was to pray.

When they started the engines, someone was standing by with a fire extinguisher. After the smoke subsided from the engines, we finally got airborne.

Vietnam

The first town we landed at was called Na Trang, which was only a short flight away. We dropped some soldiers off at this base, and we had a short waiting period, so we got coffee and doughnuts at the snack bar. There was a large beach near this base, and one of the soldiers stationed there told us that the Viet Cong and the United States military were both using it. He said that after all sides finished swimming and lying on the beach, they would start back to fighting each other. Some of the military men waiting to board the plane started asking one of the soldiers stationed there about the situation at the bases they were being assigned to on the coast. He was painting a rosy picture for most of those who asked and they seemed rather content. I finally asked him how the situation was in Quang Nai. He asked me if I was going to be assigned there. I told him, yes, I was. He said, "Sergeant, I am glad it is you going there and not me." I asked him why and he told me that they were fighting like hell then not too far from that base. I told him, "Thanks for nothing."

The next plane landing was at a town named Quinyon. We got off of the plane, and the first sergeant came out to greet the soldiers who were being stationed there. We were given Cokes, doughnuts, and coffee. It was very quite and peaceful around this base. We stayed there for about thirty minutes. I said to myself, "It is not too bad over here." I also tried to believe that the soldier at the last base was only trying to pull my leg when he mentioned about the heavy fighting around the base I was going to.

When we boarded the plane, I noticed that the flight chief who stood in the back of the plane with the phone on his ears and mouth had never spoken a word out loud since we first boarded the plane. He only talked directly over the phone to the pilot. He never showed emotions one way or the other. I named him "Iron Jaw." When we departed, we were told that we would be landing in Quang Nai in about forty-five minutes. During this run, no one said a word. In fact, it was so quiet, you could hear a rat walking on cotton. I glanced out of the window as we neared our destination, and all I could see were many trees. The plane started descending and I still could not see the air field. I heard a loud thud under the plane and the first thing that entered my mind was that we had been hit by gun fire. I found out later that it was the landing gear coming down.

Prior to landing, I finally saw this small dusty dirt landing field. It looked as if it was only one block long. The engines were still running after we landed and stopped and the flight chief hollered out, "Who is getting off in Quang Nai?" I raised my hand and said, "I am." He said, "Hurry up and get off." I told him that I would have to get my duffel bag because I had my weapon in my hands. He told me to step out of the plane. He went to the back of the plane, got my duffel bag, and threw it out on the runway and the plane took off. The whole process of the plane landing, my leaving the plane, and the plane leaving the runway took about approximately three minutes. I could not understand why the plane had stopped about thirty minutes at the last two landings and only for a very short period here.

I picked up my duffel bag and walked about fifty feet from where the plane landed. I saw a white soldier walking near some vacant buildings. He said, "Sergeant, isn't that something." I asked him what. He said, "There are about three battalions of Viet Cong soldiers about fifteen miles down the road and that is the closest they have been since I have been stationed here." I asked him what was he guarding in some of those buildings. He said there were some Viet Cong prisoners in some of those buildings. I said to myself, "With all of this action going on, I am standing here with a weapon and no ammunition."

About twenty minutes later, a soldier arrived in a jeep and asked if was I Sergeant Gurley. I answered yes, and he apologized for being so late. The entire conversation from this soldier driving back to the base was about hand grenades being thrown into jeeps carrying American soldiers while they were traveling through the crowded streets of Quang Nai. There were many Vietnamese people walking in the streets and at times, we would have to stop to keep from running over someone. During those stops, my eyes were wide open.

We finally arrived at this small base. This was an Army Signal Corp camp. There were approximately one hundred and seventy-five soldiers and about six Air Force personnel. The base seemed to be about the size of a football field, with barbed wire all around it.

I was briefed by the Army First Sergeant and walked to my living quarters. When I entered my hut, or hooch as they were called, I noticed a cement wall about twelve inches high at the entrance. I asked one of the soldiers why was it built there because it didn't make sense to me for me having to step over this barrier to get into my living quarters. I told him that it must rain pretty hard here when you have to build something to stop the rain from coming into the quarters. He said, "No, Sergeant, that wall was built to keep the snakes from crawling into your bunk."

He then proceeded to tell me about a krait snake, called the seven stepper. He said if one of those snakes bite you, you would only have time to light a cigarette because within seven steps you would be dead. He also said that one of the first things you do before getting into your bed was to check under your bedding real good before you pull your mosquito net down because snakes were known to be found in the beds of some soldiers. When he finished that introduction, he had made a believer out of me. During the period that I was stationed on this base, this was only one of the few assignments in which Air Force personnel were receiving combat pay in Vietnam. In order to earn this combat pay, you would have to spend at least seven days out of the month in the field. Some of the gung ho airmen would spend more than seven days in the field. I did not want to push my luck, so I settled for the seven days.

When I first arrived on this base, we were allowed to

go into town and visit some of the bars. Later on, intelligence reports were received that there were Viet Cong assassination squads in town looking for American soldiers. We were restricted to the base after that notice.

As time went on, you could begin to feel the tension in the air. An old Vietnamese laborer on the base was arrested and handcuffed on the base by the South Vietnamese military police because he had been identified as a major in a Viet Cong assassination squad. Some of the Army Special Forces soldiers would visit the base and state that they were surrounded at their camp and they had to fly out by helicopter to pick up more supplies and ammunition. All military personnel were briefed by the first sergeant as to what positions we were responsible for defending in case the base was attacked. Although those of us in the Air Force were working on a special project, the first sergeant said we had better forget we were in the Air Force if there was an attack. Frankly speaking, I was thinking way ahead of him.

I had now been on this base going on three months, and I was scheduled to depart from Vietnam and return to my base in the Philippines. On the day I was scheduled to leave Quang Nai, the monsoon rains had started, making it almost impossible for the plane to land on that little runway. I had sent my belongings down to the airport on a truck to be loaded on the plane if it came in. I was notified that I would have to leave another day after the rain stopped. This rain delay bothered me because one of the black Army soldiers said that during this time of rainy weather was when the Viet Cong would probably attack this base.

Around noon time on that same day, the rain stopped a little and one of the white Army warrant officers who knew me said that he was flying down to Quinyon in his helicopter. He told me that I could ride with him to Quinyon and catch the plane there that was scheduled to land in Quang Nai. I agreed to ride with him and asked one of my buddies to pick my luggage up at the airport and put it on the next plane to Tan Son Nhut Air Force Base.

When we boarded the helicopter, there were four of us aboard, including the gunner. When we began to lift off, we almost crashed into a telephone pole near the base. I figured this just wasn't my day. We finally got airborne, and headed out toward the coast, and followed the coastline until we were near Quinyon. This was my first helicopter ride and I had always pictured riding in one to be a smooth ride. Well, I was mistaken because, this was one of the roughest rides I had experienced. I could not hear anything during certain periods, which gave me the feeling that the blades had stopped turning. When we turned in from the coastline, lowering altitude as we approached the airfield, the gunner opened the door and pointed the machine gun out of the door. Later I found out that the Viet Cong would shoot at incoming and outgoing helicopters landing and departing from the airport. We finally landed safely and departed later that day on a plane to Tan Son Nhut Air Force Base. When we reached the airport outside of Saigon, it was very dark and late at night. I checked with the baggage section, and my baggage had arrived on another plane.

While we were waiting to board our plane back to the

Philippines, I noticed that the sky was lit up as if someone was setting off fireworks at the end of the runway. I was told that the Viet Cong and the military were fighting at the end of the runway. When we boarded the plane to take off, we did not have any lights on. When we reached a safe altitude and everyone sensed that we were out of harm's way, we all gave a sigh of relief. After landing at Clark Air Force Base in the Philippines, the first thing I did when we arrived at the barracks, with my "Go to Hell" hat cocked on the side of my head, was to turn on all the lights and kick every footlocker I passed. Some of the airmen who woke up due to the noise raised up in their bunks but never uttered a word. I worked on the base until I received another assignment to a base outside of Bangkok, Thailand.

Thailand

After our departure from Clark Air Force Base, we landed in Da Nang, Vietnam. When we departed we landed next on a base in Ubon, Thailand. During our stopover on this base, I noticed something that looked like fuel leaking from the plane on the ground. I notified the flight chief and the pilot as to what I had observed. After checking the plane, the pilot said it would be safe to fly the plane, but there would be no smoking on the plane. We departed the base and about twenty minutes into the flight, the flight chief lit a cigarette and started to smoke it. I walked over to him and reminded him that the pilot had said no smoking. He put the cigarette out saying that he did not hear the pilot. The plane landed at Karat Air Force Base for a short period, and finally we were on our way to Bangkok.

As we were approaching Bangkok to land, I noticed that we kept circling the airport. I heard the flight chief saying the landing gear was stuck and would not go down. We circled the field again while the flight chief attempted to lower the landing gear manually. We landed safely after getting the landing gear to respond. While we were checking into a hotel in Bangkok, I heard the pilot talking to another pilot saying that while they were in the process of trying to get the landing gear down, he had been looking for a soft rice paddy to land in.

Thailand was a very exciting country, but my biggest problem was the possibility of encountering snakes there. I remember before I departed from the Philippines, I asked one of the airmen who had been stationed in Thailand, how large were some of the snakes. He told me that the biggest snake he had seen while he was there was in a hotel in Bangkok. He said that he was living on the eleventh floor in this hotel and he looked out in the hall and saw the head of this snake coming down the hall. He then ran to look out the window and the tail of the snake was still coming through lobby on the first floor. I knew he was just joking, but I knew snakes were plentiful in this country.

During my first couple of weeks in Thailand, I stayed on the Air Force Base. Later we received per diem to rent our own apartments in Bangkok. During the time we were living on the base, when it got dark, it was not advisable to walk on the base at night due to the snakes. If you should go to town, and return to the base by taxi, you would get out at the guard shack at the front gate and call for someone to pick you up at the gate.

Many of the hotels and apartments in town were occupied by these tiny lizards crawling on the ceiling of the room. I wondered why no one tried to kill them, and I later found out that they were left alone because they ate up the other insects.

There were many places where black troops could go for entertainment in Bangkok, but many of the black troops would frequent a bar owned and operated by a black ex-GI. There were an abundance of chitterlings to be ordered and plenty of soul food. There was also plenty of fun to be had.

I believe most of the cab drivers in Thailand were racing-car drivers. I say that because when you hail down a taxicab there, they would drive so fast that they would almost scare you to death. That is the only place I have traveled in my life where I would tell the cab driver he would get a big tip if he slowed down.

One night I was working midnight shift and we were transported to work in an open-air military vehicle. The building that we worked in was built on top of a covered-up swamp. During the ride to work, we drove on a black-top road through the bushes and when the headlights were shining on the road, you could see hundreds of small snakes darting back and forth across the road. I hated to think of what would happen if someone fell off of the truck.

When we prepared to depart Thailand to return to the Philippines, the plane that we were supposed to be traveling in had noticeable bullet holes in the tail. This plane was the Air Force plane the airmen used to call "Shaky" because it was continually shaking during every flight. We were told that when it had departed Saigon, the Viet Cong shot into the tail section. I was given a choice of returning on this plane or catching the next one scheduled to return. I decided to catch the next plane, because I always had a problem when it came to riding old "Shaky" anywhere.

I arrived in the Philippines to await my next assignment. Waiting for an assignment on this base was like playing Russian roulette, because when your name came up, you never knew where you would be sent. You stood a chance of going back to Vietnam or to any hole you did not want to be in.

During the period of time I stayed on the Philippine Islands, I had the opportunity to meet some of the Nigritoe people living there. They were members of dwarfish Negroid people of the Islands. They were small in stature, but to me they looked more like black people in America. I was told that they had a king and they had the privilege to do many things on Clark Air Force Base that other Philippine people were not allowed to do. I understand that this was an agreement the United States Government made with them after World War II because of their fierce fighting against the Japanese army during the war. They knew the jungle well and used poison darts and bow and arrows accurately. Some people say that they are the true Philippine natives of the Islands.

They were allowed to sell trinkets on Clark Air Force Base, to the military personnel. They would sell you bow and arrows, knives, blow dart guns, and many other items made by the group. They would also let you have them on credit if you did not have the money to pay at the time of purchase. And something always amazed me during this transaction with the troops because, on payday, no one ever forgot to pay the bill.

After our spending a few weeks on Clark Air Force Base in the Philippines, there was a notification issued that two volunteers were needed for replacements in Thailand. I quickly accepted one of the positions, because, considering all I experienced over there, I really enjoyed my last assignment. After receiving my orders, I found out that Airman Johnson would accompany me on this assignment. We boarded the plane and landed at Ton Son Nhut Air Force Base for a short stop and then departed for our destination in Thailand.

During this flight, we were not allowed to fly over Cambodia, so we headed out over the South China Sea and headed up the Gulf of Thailand toward Bangkok. Prior to this flight and other airplane flights, most of my buddies knew that I did not like to fly and they used to joke with me about this. My phobia about flying started after the engine on one of the planes caught on fire on a flight to Thule, Greenland, and that fear grew with every flight I took afterwards. Even Airman Johnson who was on this flight with me knew that I had a phobia about flying. He was kidding with me when we boarding the plane about how afraid I was about flying. I had a habit of always buckling my seat belt and never unloosening it until the plane landed.

As we were flying along and we were about forty-five

minutes out before touchdown at Bangkok, we were just finishing lunch and I glanced out of the window and noticed that we were approaching some thick black clouds. All of a sudden, the plane started falling as if there was no air in the sky. I just knew that the Grim Reaper had finally caught up with me. I had experienced air pockets before, but it seemed as though we were falling farther than the distance of some pockets. The plates and cups that we were using that still had food on them and coffee were spilling on the ceiling and the wall of the plane. We had Japanese stewardesses on board, and they started screaming and hollering. When I heard the stewardesses scream, I knew this was the real thing because, they are usually calm in a situation like this.

Finally we hit solid air and the plane started flying smoothly again. I noticed that Airman Johnson had his fingernails dug in my right leg. After we all regained our composure, I looked over at him and said, "Take your hands off of my leg and don't you ever tell anyone that you are not afraid to fly anymore."

After landing in Bangkok safely, we were provided transportation to Ubon, Thailand, that was located north of Bangkok, near the Laotian border. We were sort of like in the boondocks. It was so quiet at night, it seemed as if you could hear the sound of every insect imaginable. It was quite a contrast from the city of Bangkok. During my first week at this location, I stayed on the base. It was not a big base, but you could see that they were continually building barracks to make it larger.

Eventually, I moved into one of the one-room huts located across this big field from the base. This big field that was covered with high grass separated our huts from main base. I never crossed this field at night when I was going to work on the base because I did not want to run into any snakes. To reach the base by using the main roads leading there would take you about twenty minutes. Taking a short cut across this field would take about five minutes. I watched several airmen taking the short cut across the field for about a week. I finally decided that I would take my chances. During my first walk, I was a little apprehensive but, as time passed, I forgot all about the snakes.

A few weeks later, there was a terrible storm. The rain and wind blew some of the power lines down, and we were without lights in our huts. While some of the airmen were trying to find out how to get some lighting in the area, someone hollered that they had seen a snake. One of the airmen had a flashlight and asked me to look over towards the hut where he was shining his light. I looked over there and what I saw made a believer out of me. I saw this huge snake that looked greenish and the body was just as round as a fifty-five gallon gasoline drum. Some of the Thai people were hitting the snake with sticks, but the snake was still crawling slowly under one of the huts. The next day I ceased walking across that field permanently for the duration of my tour of duty in Ubon.

I noticed that many more barracks were being constructed on the base. It was rumored that we would be getting some more airmen on the base. Several days later, I looked up at the sky and it looked like the sun was dark because of the many planes that were circling to land on the airfield. After the planes landed, we could we could see hundreds of airmen unloading. This was a welcomed sight, seeing all of those reinforcements because the Thai Army was pulling most of the guard duty on the base, and we were aware that those troops had not been tested in battle.

After the troops landed, I noticed that there were many black airmen in the group. I was very glad to meet many of them because they would tell me about the latest news from different parts of the States. There were black airmen from New York, Chicago, Washington, D.C., and many other cities back home.

Most of these airmen were part of the support group assigned to keep the planes in good condition so they could accomplish their mission.

When these fighter planes departed from the airfield, I had no idea where they were headed. In fact, I figured they were mostly training for future planning. I finally found out what was going on when I received communications that some planes were returning to the base to land and my job was to contact the Fire department, Ambulance, Chaplain, Commanding Officer, and other emergency personnel. My little wooden hut was located adjacent to the runway, and I could look out of my window and see planes returning on fire, black smoke gushing out of the engine with some crash landing and exploding on impact. Trying to contact the emergency personnel and looking out of the window to see if one of those planes were headed for my office was a dangerous situation to be in. During the period when I observed planes returning after bombing raids, most of the pilots who returned and crashed landed were rescued by emergency personnel.

I remember calling back to Quang Ngai, Vietnam, on the military phone to find out how things were going over there. When one of the airman answered the phone, I identified myself and the airman said, "Sergeant Gurley, you are a lucky man to be away from here now." He told me to listen for a while after he held the phone out of the window. I could hear gunfire, and it sounded as if bombs were being dropped. He said, "They are fighting not too far from the airfield." I wished him the best of luck and said a prayer for him.

Seven
Westover Air Force Base, England; Torrejon AFB, Spain

Westover Air Force Base

A few weeks later, my replacement arrived and I departed Ubon for my trip back to the Philippines. After arriving back to my home base, I received my military orders assigning me to Westover Air Force Base in Springfield, Massachusetts. This was my first tour of duty being assigned to the Strategic Air Command (SAC). This was an outfit in which you soldiered or you suffered the consequence. That meant if you did not perform on your job as expected or better, you could be demoted or discharged from the service. I enjoyed being in this elite outfit because, I have always liked to soldier. I hated being in an outfit that had poor leadership.

After being in the Strategic Air Command for over a year, a request was forwarded to my squadron for someone needed for an overseas assignment. The person considered for this assignment was required to be experienced and to have outstanding capabilities in all aspects of his military career. I applied for the assignment reluctantly but hopeful that I would receive it. My application was selected, and I was assigned to a small base in England.

England

I arrived in England during the first part of November 1966. The base I was assigned to was part of the Strategic Area Command. I was very pleased with this assignment. However, never in my wildest dreams could I have envisioned what was about to shape my future in this squadron.

My first impression after being introduced to the officers and enlisted men on this base was the closeness of the personnel stationed there. I also noticed that there were only a few black airmen in this squadron. The atmosphere felt like one of those "good ole boys" outfits. I do not believe they expected to get a black replacement for this duty. I really felt that I was not accepted here. I tried very hard to be friendly with everybody. I always kept a smile on my face regardless of what the situation was. I really wanted to succeed in this outfit because I liked the assignment.

During the first two or three weeks on the base, I was still waiting for the arrival of my automobile. One of the black airmen told me that the Coasters, a rock and roll group, was going to perform in London and he asked me whether I wanted to go. I told him I would like to go, but I didn't have any transportation. He told me that he was driving, and if I wanted to, I could ride with him. I agreed and we departed for London that night.

The show was over around 5:00 A.M. the next morning, and we started on our trip back to the base. I noticed that the fog was getting heavy on the way back. There were four of us in the car and two of the airmen were asleep. I kept dozing off and on, but I kept asking the driver if he could see the road okay, and he replied that he could. In England, you drive on the opposite side of the road compared to the way you drive in the States. The drive from London to our base was approximately fifty miles. I fell asleep for a short period, and when I opened my eyes, I noticed that we had been involved in a head-on collision.

The driver was standing outside of the car and was bleeding from his head and his chest. The airman who was riding in the front passenger side seemed to be unconscious, lying back on the seat. I felt a bump on my head and my ankles felt sore in the front part of them. The airman sitting in the back seat next to me did not receive a scratch. I shook the airman in the front seat because he looked as if he was dead. He finally regained consciousness and got out of the car. The ambulance arrived and transported us to the hospital. We were finally released after they found out that we did not have any serious injuries. We were very lucky because the car was a total loss.

When we arrived back on the base later that morning, I was informed that the Commanding Officer wanted to see me in his office. When I reported to his office, he never asked me how was I feeling. He only asked me to explain what happened in reference to the accident. He did not ask me was I hurt or how was I feeling. I gave him an explanation as to what had happened. He told me that due to the fact that I was the highest ranking airman riding in the car, he was going to put that incident report in my records and he would be keeping an eye on me. I tried to explain to him that the automobile belonged to the airman who was driving and that I did not have any control over the circumstances. He said that did not make any difference.

I knew then that I would have to cover my back side from here on in. I remembered what an old black sergeant had told me once when I first entered the military. He said, "Son, regardless of what happens to you, always keep a little black book handy where you can jot down incidents so you can remember them later on." He said, "You can't keep all of that information in your head and you might need it one day." I knew that this was what I had to do in order to survive now.

I was assigned as a shift supervisor during my first week in the squadron. This was very unusual because normally, most airmen were required to work several weeks during the day shifts to get acquainted with the system prior to being assigned as shift supervisor.

During the month of December 1966, I was told by my direct supervisor that I was doing an outstanding job as supervisor of a shift after taking over the shift in such a short notice. He also told me that there was an airman assigned to my shift who had presented problems to other shift supervisors and he wanted me to be aware of it. I had noticed that at times when I would ask this white airman to perform certain duties, he would get very angry and start kicking the machines. I believe what he resented most was a black sergeant giving him orders. I began to counsel this airman in a tactful manner, explaining to him that we were all there to complete a job, and orders he received from me were passed down by higher authority to be completed. After this encounter, he began to work very hard to accomplish his assigned duties.

I was not aware that this white airman in question was on the squadron bowling team. I was also not aware that the Communication Superintendent was on the bowling team. I was advised by my assistant who happened to be white and not in that bowling circle that this airman would make negative remarks about me during some of the bowling games. He said the airman would say that I was not like the rest of the non-commissioned officers and he did not like me and did not want to work for me. I immediately notified my direct supervisor about those negative remarks. The airman was called in by my supervisor and asked about the remarks. He told my supervisor that he just did not like me, period.

The superintendent entered the office shortly after the conversation with the airman, and he was made aware of the remarks mentioned by him. I was advised by the superintendent that the airman would be leaving soon to go home and he wanted him to get a good performance report. He also stated that maybe it was my supervision that made the airman act the way he had been acting. I could not believe that I was hearing the superintendent correctly because, this was the same airman who gave the rest of the shift supervisors problems before I arrived and no one had attempted to correct him because he was a personal friend of the superintendent. Now that I was put into the position of trying to correct his attitude, I found myself in a very awkward position.

During the month of May 1967, I was informed by my supervisor that the airman in question would be relieved of duty from my shift, although he was performing better than he had ever performed on shift. I was told that the reason he was being relieved was to give him a break so he could work straight days before he departed for the States.

On June 6, 1967, I was asked by my supervisor to excuse another airman off of my shift to play baseball. I informed him that we had a Strategic Air Command exercise coming up and there were only three airmen on duty. I suggested that maybe one of the day workers could fill in for this airman so we could be sure the center would be fully manned. He told me that the squadron wanted these airmen excused during all sports events. I excused the airman, leaving the center with an undermanned crew.

When I reported for work the next day, which was June 7, 1967, my supervisor told me that I did not let the airman off from duty to play ball. He said the airman had to go to the superintendent in order to get off. I called the airman in to verify that I did let him off to play ball. My supervisor told me that I was not going along with the program in reference to letting the ball players off. I explained to my supervisor that I was responsible for anything that happened while I was on duty and I was being forced to release certain airmen to play ball regardless of whether I got replacements for these individuals or not. I added that if there was a security violation, I would be held responsible for those actions and not him.

On June 14, 1967, I was ordered to report to the officer in charge and the superintendent. I was told by them that I was not going along with the program, and I was using my rank too much. I really believed that they really wanted something to happen on my shift so they could start procedures to remove me, period. I asked both of them to at least give me the fair judgment of defending myself against these false accusations. They refused to listen to anything I was saying. Later, I asked my direct supervisor as to why did they call me into the front office without going through him first. He admitted that it was wrong and he would look into it.

On September 4, 1967, I was made aware that my assistant supervisor had been called into the superintendent's office and was asked how was he getting along on my shift and was I giving him any trouble. My assistant supervisor was a white sergeant from Georgia. He informed me that he told him he never felt more at ease on Sergeant Gurley's shift than he does now. He said the superintendent said he could not understand that. There were others on the shift who were also questioned about how they felt about me. Later on I visited the superintendent's office and requested to be relieved of my duties as shift supervisor and to be assigned to duty on straight days if he was so critical of my supervisory capabilities. He told me that he was unable to give me a day job because they were all taken.

During this turbulent period, I was called in several times to see my supervisor, the superintendent and the officer in charge, but I had never received any counseling during the entire time since arriving on this base. I had asked for a transfer out of the squadron and was told that they would try to transfer me as an overage. I was told that an overage transfer was requested, but it came back disapproved.

It was now the month of November 1967, and I realized it was about time that I should be receiving an airman's performance report. I checked with the personnel clerk to see if it was put in my files. I was told that it had been written a few days earlier and forwarded on to Headquarters for the Strategic Air Command. My direct supervisor was responsible for writing my airman performance report, and it was mandatory that he discuss it with me before it was forwarded to the superintendent. This was not done. I was never briefed, and it was never mentioned that it was even written. I requested a copy of my performance report from my supervisor, and he said he did not have a copy of it, but I should check with the superintendent. I visited the superintendent's office, and he let me look at a rough draft of a copy he pulled out of his desk drawer. After reviewing this draft copy, I now realized why everything was so secretive.

My supervisor entered the following remarks on my performance report: "STRENGTHS: Sergeant Gurley is a self-assured and confident non-commissioned officer. He remains calm during periods of stress and can generally be relied on to carry his duties through to completion. RECOMMENDED IMPROVEMENT AREAS: Sergeant Gurley has a tendency to misinterpret some instructions and to resist constructive criticism; he seems to take this constructive criticism as a personal attack upon himself rather than a correction to a deviation from established in-station policy. I have personally counseled Sergeant Gurley concerning this deficiency, but his attitude remains virtually unchanged."

The superintendent entered the following remarks: "Sergeant Gurley has a positive attitude toward duty and military affairs; however, he does seem to have a tendency to deviate from established procedures and do things 'his way' no matter what the outcome. I have discussed this situation with Sergeant Gurley but have found that he requires a lot of reasons and/or convincing before he believes the procedure/methods are correct. I noticed during the exercise that Sergeant Gurley performed his duties as shift supervisor adequately and followed all instructions given to him to the letter."

The officer in charge wrote: "I believe this report to be completely fair and objective."

After reading and thinking about this negative performance report, I realized that I had served eighteen years in the military and thirteen of those years in grade as a Staff Sergeant. On my records I never had a court martial and I have never been absent without leave (AWOL) during my entire military career. I knew then that it was time for me to contact some one outside of this organization to get help before they ruined my career.

On November 21, 1967, I sent a letter to United States Inspector General's office in the Pentagon, also sending copies to the Strategic Air Command Inspector General and the NAACP in Washington, D.C. In the letter, I explained about the personnel and operational problems in the squadron. I also requested a transfer out of the squadron.

Prior to November 21, 1967, I had requested and was granted permission to work two shifts for another sergeant on another shift and in return he would work two midnight shifts for me on the 25th and 26thof November. On the 28th of November, I was called in by the Commanding Officer to explain why was I absent from those two midnight shifts. I explained to him that my supervisor was aware of why I did not work those shifts. He listened, but he insisted on sending me a short letter making the incident a part of my record.

On December 4, 1967, I received a letter of reprimand for failure to coordinate with my supervisor prior to working two midnight shifts. It stated on the letter that the letter would be filed in my mobility folder for a period of ninety days. It also stated that I was to acknowledge receipt and understanding no later than December 6, 1967. My answer to the reprimand was, "The charges contained in the letter of reprimand are completely false. My supervisor was notified prior to my changing shift. My signature is signed only for the acknowledgment and receipt of the letter."

On December 14, 1967, I received a second endorsement from the Commanding Officer stating, "On November 28, 1967, I talked to you in my office concerning the incident described in the basic letter. At that time, I told you that I was going write a short letter making the incident a matter of record sent you. At that time, you did not state that you had notified your supervisor prior to changing shift. Request your reasons for withholding this vital information from me." I thought the Commanding Officer had lost his mind. I did not answer the request.

During this period, the organization had received notification that I had filed a complaint with the Inspector General. I was ordered to report to the officer in charge who was in the office of the superintendent. I repeated again my concern about the unfair treatment that I was receiving in the organization. I also requested that other shift supervisors should be questioned about numerous incidents that had happened on different shifts, and the truth would come to life. A meeting was held with certain shift supervisors. My immediate supervisor was relieved of his duties and replaced by another supervisor. With that action, I felt as though my point had been proven to a certain degree, but I was still concerned about my negative performance report.

I received a letter from the Inspector General's Office in the Pentagon requesting that I give more details and facts to substantiate the allegations in my letter dated November 21,1967. I opened my little black book with all of the information that I had compiled in reference to the unfair treatment I had received in this organization, wrote a long letter to the Inspector General's office in the Pentagon, and forwarded a copy to the NAACP in Washington, D.C. giving details and facts in reference to my allegations.

The response from the Pentagon was that further inquiry was made into the operations at my squadron and other allegations included in my letter. The letter also stated that an inquiry was made by a qualified officer from another station. It was stipulated that the inquiry revealed that there were several changes in duty assignments during December, which appeared to have improved the management and operation of the center. It further stated that my duty assignment was changed and I had been reassigned to another section under a different supervisor. They believed that those actions would resolve many of my problems.

They instructed me that the only way I could have the airman performance report removed from my records was to ask for an appeal through procedures established in an Air Force manual. The last section of the letter stated that, "Though there does appear to be a basis for appealing the airman performance report, there is no indication that personnel at my base have any intent to treat you unfairly or duly harass you. There is no established basis for reassigning you. The possibility of reassigning you was considered, however, but no vacancies exist in your specialty in the overseas area. Therefore, no further action will be taken on your reassignment."

This letter from the Pentagon was a shocking response because the letter I had forwarded to them was well written and there was documentation attached with highly significant facts to my allegations. My main concern about this letter from the Pentagon was that it would put me in a position that would create more harassment by my superiors with no one to turn to for help.

While I was thinking about what other avenue I could explore to get some help, a few days later after receiving that reply, an Inspecting General's team of inspectors arrived at the base unexpectedly. Everyone in the organization was caught by surprise. It seemed as though everyone was in a panic mode. The colonel who was in charge of the team called me up to his command office, advised me that he was here with the team to investigate my allegations, and asked me to explain one of the paragraphs I had written in my letter. After I explained to him what I meant in the letter, he told me I could depart because the inspection would now begin.

During the second day of the inspection, one of the inspectors mentioned that he had found enough violations. Almost all of my allegations had been proven to be correct. The inspectors departed the base after being there approximately three days.

About one week later, I received a letter from my Commanding Officer stating, "This is to inform you that the recent investigation of your charges concerning an unfair and prejudicial airman performance report has been reviewed by Headquarters Strategic Air Command. Headquarters has concluded that there is adequate justification for you to request that the airman performance report be voided and removed from your records. I have instructed my staff administrative officer to render every assistance to you in preparation of this report. He will advise you, secure typing support and provide general instructions in this matter." This letter alleviated some of my concerns, but I really wanted a transfer out of that organization.

I received the assistance in requesting that the airman performance be removed from my records. After reconsidering all that had happened to me in this organization, I decided that the only way I was going to get a transfer was to take some drastic measures. I stayed up for several nights until the wee hours of the morning, writing a letter to Senator Robert F. Kennedy. When I finished with the letter, I put all of my attachments concerning my situation, explaining to him what I had been experiencing in the organization. I also noted that I was advised that I would be unable to get a transfer out of that organization. I asked him if he would assist me in getting a transfer out of this hostile environment.

During this period, my Commanding Officer received a letter from Headquarters, Strategic Air Command, stating, "Airman Performance report has been voided by the Report Review Board. Request the following actions be accomplished: a. Remove the voided report from the field record group and destroy. b. Insert AF Form 77a in the field record group. c. Return supporting documents to the applicant. d. Advise applicant when you have completed the above." A copy of this letter was also forwarded to me.

Shortly after this action, I was ordered to report to my Commanding Officer. When I reported to his office, I was informed that information had been received by him that I would be getting transferred out of the organization. He said that I would be transferred to an air base in Spain. He asked me why didn't I tell him about what was going on in the organization. I told him that I had tried to discuss the situation with him several times, but he just would not listen to me.

I departed England by boat across the English Channel. The water in the channel was rather choppy, but it was way better than flying. Incidentally, I chose the boat trip over flying.

Torrejon AFB, Spain

We landed on the coast of France and boarded a train for our trip to Paris. We arrived in Paris around 9:00 P.M. There was a layover in Paris for approximately three hours before the train would depart for Madrid, Spain. My final destination after arriving in Madrid would be Torrejon Air Force Base located on the outskirts. During the time I waited at the train station, I ventured out to view Paris at night, and it was a very beautiful sight. There seemed to be every nationality in the world mingling within that area. I treated myself to a glass of French wine and ate plenty of French bread.

I boarded the train around midnight for my overnight journey into Spain. The train was rather crowded, and one almost had to struggle to find a seat. People were packed in most of the compartments, with many sleeping on those canvas-type bunk beds where three people could sleep, one over the other. I finally fell asleep on one of the stationary seats, and when I woke up the next morning, we were miles across the French border into Spain. It seemed as though I was starving on this particular morning, and I wanted to order some breakfast. I was told by one of the passengers that someone would be around to take my order soon. This was around 10:00 A.M. when I was given this information, and I did not receive any food until approximately 1:00 P.M. I was surprised when shortly after eating my breakfast I was served my lunch and my dinner. I thought this was rather strange, but I was told that this was the way things were.

When we arrived in Madrid, transportation was waiting to pick us up for a short ride to the base.

When I reported to my Duty Officer the next day, we were both very surprised. He had been one of the inspectors assigned to investigate my allegations prior to my leaving England. We both shook hands and laughed about the incident. He also advised me that if there was anything he could help me with, to feel free to contact him at any time.

This was a huge base, and there were many black airmen stationed here. Although the base was integrated, black airmen preferred being with their own. From the clubs on the base to the little bars downtown in Madrid, the black troops hung out with their own. From my personal view, I hung out with my own because I was tired of being in a fighting posture all of the time. I knew that if I visited some of those bars where Southern white airmen hung out there was a strong possibility that someone was going to get hurt and it was not going to be me. I also realized that most of the time when there *are* racial incidents, the black trooper gets the short end of the stick even if he was right. So rather than go through those changes, I hung with my own.

There were several national and international incidents that occurred during my tour of duty in Spain. One of them was the assassination of Robert Kennedy, and the other was the landing of the Astronauts on the moon. One was a very sad occasion, and the other was a very happy one.

Most of my time off was spent on the base visiting many of the black married couples living on the base. On the weekends, it seemed as though there was always a party or a cook-out to attend. When I decided to venture out into the city of Madrid, especially in some of the bars, people were looking at you as if you came from outer space. Now there were a few bars that one could visit where most of the patrons were black. Most of these establishments I used to call "the hole in the wall." That is what they appeared to be to me. Some of the more exclusive clubs in town would make you feel as though you did not belong there, although they never came right out and said it. It was like being in an atmosphere where you knew there was racism, but you could not put your hands on it.

I will never forget the day I received some tickets to go to a bull fight in Madrid. I was really excited because previously, I had only seen bull fights on televisions back in the States, and now I was getting the opportunity to see one in person. When I arrived at the stadium, there were thousands of people lining up to get in. If I did not know I was stationed in Spain, I would have sworn that I was waiting to go in to see the Redskins play at RFK stadium in Washington, D.C.

The matador dressed elegantly in his beautiful decorated attire entered the ring to the roar of approval from thousands of his fans seated in the stands. This big black bull was finally released from behind one of the iron gates at the far end of the stadium. The matador made a few slick moves, and the crowd roared in approval. The bull missed the matador on his first rush, but when he came back for the second rush, I could not believe what I was seeing. This was the first bull fight I had witnessed, and the bull had just gored the matador and tossed him into the air with blood flying everywhere. Many of the attendants working in the bull ring tried to lure the bull away from the matador, but it was too late. His mangled body lay still in a pool of blood. This scene still remains in the back of my mind, and I will never forget it. I have never attended another bull fight since.

Many of the black airmen and their families stationed on Torrejon Air Force Base would hold a party or celebration when one of their friends was scheduled to return to the United States. They would all go down to the air terminal on their date of departure to wish them a happy journey. It was the same routine on the trip back to McGuire Air Force Base in New Jersey. You knew that the plane would depart Torrejon Air Force Base and arrive in McGuire AFB eight hours later.

After seeing so many friends off and attending so many departing parties, it finally became my time to have a party in my honor prior to departing Spain.

I tried to get a boat reservation for my return trip to the States, but I was told that I did not qualify. I really did not want to fly because flying was just not my cup of tea. Well, after trying all avenues to get out of this flight, I finally accepted reality and that was if I wanted to get home, I would have to fly or retire over there. I prepared myself mentally and boarded the plane for my trip back to the States.

Prior to boarding the plane, we were notified that this plane would be flying a different route back to the States. I said to myself, after watching many of my friends leaving this base with a direct flight to New Jersey in eight hours, they have now decided they want to change this route with George Gurley as one of the passengers. We were told that we would depart Torrejon Air Force Base and fly to Rota, Spain, which would be south of Madrid. We would then pick up some sailors and fly them to Quonset Point, Rhode Island, and then continue on to McGuire Air Force Base in New Jersey.

When we arrived at Rota Air Force Base, we departed the plane and were transported to some of the transit barracks on the base. During this period, in 1969, there had been turmoil back in the States with the assassination of Martin Luther King, the riots, and the assassination of Robert Kennedy.

I vividly remember that some of the young black sailors wearing their huge Afros had a serious confrontation with some white sailors, and they were arrested and were confined in the barracks. I discussed the incident with some of the black sailors and was told that they were not taking any more insults from white people and they were ready to go to jail. You could tell that this was a new breed of young blacks.

We finally boarded the plane and departed for Quonset Point, Rhode Island. There were approximately three hundred people on board this plane, and my main thoughts were to get to our final destination as soon as possible. The flight was pretty smooth until we were about forty-five minutes away from landing at Quonset Point. All of a sudden, the plane started shaking violently as if there was an explosion on the plane. Quite naturally, my heart was in my mouth, but I never showed signs of panic. I looked around the plane and some folks were praying silently and others looked petrified with their eyes staring straight towards the ceiling. My first thoughts were, if we land in the frigid waters, we would freeze to death in a matter of seconds. Although the light came on displaying the "fasten your seat belts" and "no smoking," the pilot never mentioned to the passengers what was going on. I am kind of glad that he didn't.

We landed at Quonset Point safely, and the sailors we picked up in Rota, Spain departed for their destination. We then departed for our destination in McGuire Air Force Base in New Jersey. After a short flight, we landed in the State of New Jersey. I was scheduled to catch a flight out of McGuire to Washington, D.C., but I did not want to press my luck anymore. I decided to catch a cab to the train station, board a train, and spend the balance of my time on the ground.

I was assigned to Bolling Air Force Base in Washington, D.C., until my retirement where I received my Honorable Discharge after serving twenty years and fourteen days faithfully in the United States Armed Forces.